TICKET TO THE UNKNOWN

TICKET TO THE UNKNOWN

JINA VALENTINE

TABLE OF CONTENTS

PART I: ALOÏSE'S WRITING

Notes from the First Encounter with Aloïse's Texts

Mute Word Blind Vision

Texts and Translations

Cryptophasic Idioglassia: Lexicon

PART II: READING ALOÏSE

Life of Aloïse Corbaz

Against Interpretation

Genesis

NOTES FROM THE FIRST
ENCOUNTER WITH ALOÏSE'S TEXTS

LETTRE À GUILLAUME II

*I'd love to know what was erased, and when and why
it was replaced. "Merveilleuse," is erased mostly, and is
replaced with "suprenante et adorable."*

NOËL DE SAINT ROSAIRE

*Noël is flush with notations between lines and in the
margins. Words are frequently underlined and written
in very tight script ... though it is all in ink, one can discern between the 'original text,' and subsequent notations, revisions, and erasures. In addition there's the*

text which serves as a title or a marquee "Mahaim mon phare Bonte volé à render recteur de l'université...." and diagonally "Albert Mahaim." The text in the margins on the verso is overflow from the first page ... the text under-lay is in pencil.

À MADEMOISELLE ROSINE

Reading Aloïse' texts transcribed, we're immediately exposed to the content of the text, but completely without the image of it—the impression of it as it was spontaneously birthed onto the page. The flow of the language is lost. In particular words that fill entire lines: "immortal," or "comme." There are few words that are retraced, for added emphasis, or in reconsideration of their meaning and placement on the page. Or in the way the spaces are darkened in some areas to lend definition to the rendered object—in drawing, some portions of the drawing are over-drawn; in writing some words receive the same treatment. DIEU / DEUS EX MACHINA in capitals, and the serifs of the letters used to underline other words, or themselves. But, in general, one could say that the style of handwriting is muttering as écriture—it is written as it was heard.

BILLET À L'INCONNUE

The image framing the text is blue watercolor, a duotone print of a tree branch with flowers which breaks up the original text inscribed by Aloïse. Her text rarely overwrites the image and is written in all directions, as though the negative space defined by the print dictated the direction of her text. Turning the paper 90 degrees produces an additional expanse of empty space to be filled with text.

LE SOLEIL DE LA MAPPEMONDE DE SANS-SOUCI

What's immediately curious about this text is the close attention paid to rendering the woman's face—a single line forms the contours and features, the hair—while the more fluidly, vigorously rendered environment seems to have poured out of the pencil. The application of graphite buckles the paper (in the outline of the architecture) and the space between architectural elements is filled on the left side in straight even strokes—the right side is cross-hatched. The rendering of the "architectural elements" suggests fabric or curtains. All of this is on grid-paper, folded three times in the middle, which seems to contradict the apparent spontaneity of production. On the verso, the original writing is in pen—the secondary writing is overlaid in graphite pencil. The writing in ink is very small, tight cursive which seems to have been written in an earlier, calmer state—the later overlay is loopy and almost indecipherable.

MUTE WORD BLIND VISION

Even through the cotton gloves required to handle fragile archived arti-facts, the tactility of the paper was so immediate. Having read, trans-lated, and studied the structure of Aloïse's writings in advance of wit-nessing them firsthand, the sensation of actually *holding these texts* was one of pure elation. The individual pages were soft and slightly worn from handling, folding, erasures and use. The fibers, loosened and broken in places, suggested that the paper had aged during the writing and subsequent readings by its author. It was clear that these writings had never existed as staid words on a page: the text and the paper itself were living entities. Aloïse pilfered paper from the waste bin to create her earlier works, so one might think that this detritus material had degraded before reaching her hands. But the revisions, effacings, and creases are signs that writing took place over the course of multiple sessions, and that the papers were carried around in between.

Aloïse's writings vividly evidence the process buried within the text. As a paper-maker fascinated by the idea of the palimpsest (a text erased and rewritten *ad infinitum* to conserve material), I find her use of textual layering extremely compelling. In her work one can see an ongoing value war between content and material scarcity. These are manuscripts, literally, "handwritten text," and it is clear that the text and Aloïse were equally judicious with the expenditure of material—they operate in calligraphic collaboration. The spatial limitations of the paper prescribe the potential textual territories, as well as the direction, density, and size of the letters themselves. And textual accretions, the accumulation of marks on the page, serve to further delimit what space remains for expansion.

In the multi-directional, layered writing one can also see Aloïse fighting against the material inadequacy of a two-dimensional page: some words span entire lines, some lines contain the content of a paragraph; sentences are erased and replaced with a word or two; the serif functions in the liminal space between drawn form, letter, and typographic emphasis. The handling of the page suggests that the paper is a space to contain writing, rather than one upon which to record and communicate a sentiment. It becomes apparent that, unlike most texts, Aloïse's primary objective was not one of extroverted communication—from writer to eventual reader—but rather the articulation of an internal monologue. Aloïse was engaged in direct transcription of words as they appeared to her, or as she heard them.

Nietzsche writes in *Twilight of the Idols* that artists in a frenzied state—who cannot help but create—had best position themselves in a space where hands, not quills are developed. *Hands, not quills* suggests that the artist ought to grapple with the task at hand rather than adorning it with eloquence, flowery, and twee. Had Aloïse recorded her sentiments on a typewriter, or written on pristine, lined paper; had her sentiment not propelled her vision forward; had she lingered or labored over the "correct" form of the prose transcribed, wouldn't it have compromised the immediacy of the text itself? In developing *hands not quills*, Aloïse directly transcribes words onto a found object, grappling with it, turning it, wearing it away through her touch. And the result is one in which the process of translating oral language to written language—*taming language* to fit into regular, linear pattern on a page—is renounced. The spoken word, *la parole*, is transcribed directly onto form, omitting the usual process of reduction and refinement.

The resulting immediacy of the language retains all the sensuality of spoken word, and illustrates the process involved in its transcription.

In *La Voleuse de Mappemonde*,[1] by Aloïse's friend and biographer Dr. Jacqueline Porret-Forel, Aloïse's texts are carefully transposed from the original manuscripts. A few images of the original texts provide an idea of the form on paper. Porret-Forel explains that the process of reading Aloïse's texts for the first time involved carefully scanning each line, gleaning what was comprehensible, and reading until another line made sense.[2] By stitching together patches of rationality within a skein of nebulous and often difficult to decipher script, Jacqueline found her footing. From there, she navigated through the gnarlier passages of still-coded text. The *inframince*, that in-between space of Duchampian thought, required the most rigorous knowledge of her subject. Porret-Forel attained a particular acuity for reading that which would appear opaque to most. This skill manifests in her ability to decipher those handwritten words whose identity verges on ambiguity. Intuiting meaning in those liminal spaces requires a sturdy knowledge of the author, her idiomatic language, and the overall meaning of the text itself.

Foucault writes, "each age has its own particular way of putting language together, because of its different groupings."[3] If the ability to recognize particular groupings has to do with a shared context, Porret-Forel was uniquely suited to the task of deciphering Aloïse because both are *Vaudoises* (from the Vaud Canton of Switzerland) and Porret-Forel is just one generation removed from Aloïse. The myriad references to specific places in Lausanne, the free association with then-popular cultural references, and Aloïse's now-antiquated use of the Swiss-French language required an intimate acquaintance with the place, the era, and the author herself. The transposed texts faithfully record the written words of each manuscript and Porret-Forel has annotated the places where words are underlined, or scribbled in the margin or in super/subscript. In cases where a narrative turns ninety degrees, or disappears onto the verso, or is interwoven into a previous

---

1   Jacqueline Porret-Forel, *La Voleuse de Mappemonde* (Gèneve: Éditions Zoé, 2004).

2   Muriel Edelstein, *Sans Souci, l'art d'Aloïse* (Paris, Long Par Court, Absynthe Productions 2000), 54'.

3   Michel Foucault, *The Order of Things* (London: Routledge, 1989), 55.

statement, she has taken pains to iron out the language, or to structure the prose into a progression better comprehensible for the reader. In the rare case where a word or phrase proves too unwieldy to decode, it's replaced with [...]. Facing the actuality of these texts and attempting to piece together words without Porret-Forel's transcription, one begins to get a sense of the task she tackled.

But perhaps Porret-Forel's texts sacrifice materiality in the interest of legibility. In *Détournement de l'écriture*, an examination of the writings of Art Brut artists, Michel Thévoz[4] writes, "the typed character protects verbal expression against the idiomatic deformations of manuscripts ... [it] exempts the word of all corporeality and it assures the most perfect significative transparence."[5] Thévoz suggests that while they enable a smooth reading, Porret-Forel's transcriptions also dispossess the text of its tactility; they eliminate the encumbrance of the hieroglyphic, scripted word. The text, stripped of its "primitive body" (the gesture, the tone), is normalized or neutered, forfeiting much of its sensuality and all of its graphic qualities. The words themselves are laid bare at the expense of the corporeality of the written manuscript. It could be reasoned that the visibility of the textual body and the articulability of the typographic text are equally significant, but entirely *compossible*[6] states. Thévoz refers to this dilemma in his discussion of "semantic aphasia," stating that in this verbal metastasis, "the visibility does not play second to the legibility, it spirits it away; the legibility doesn't caution the visibility, it confounds it: they are each other's para sites."[7]

Thévoz argues that the Gutenberg era's renewed interest in the manuscript (in drawing, in evidence of handling) is a reaction against the neutered content-only text of popular media; this refers to the typed word, the online text, word as digital form stripped of evidence of the

---

4   Thévoz was the first director of the Art Brut Collection, a friend of Jean Dubuffet, a professor at the University of Lausanne, and is an art theorist and historian.
5   Michel Thévoz, *Détournement de l'écriture* (Paris: Editions de Minuit, 1989), 12.
6   This term originally appears in Deleuze & Guattari's *Cinema I* and refers to the simultaneous compatibility and disjunction of visual and aural qualities of film, two qualities that are interrelated, but defiant of any potential coexistence.
7   Michel Thévoz, *Écriture en Délire* (Lausanne: Collection d'Art Brut, 2004), 13.

human hand.[8] In fact, contemporary artists have long sought out the points where the corporeality of written word merges with drawing— or where, as in Art Brut writings[9], the opacification of the text's meaning limits the reader to a consideration of form. But in Aloïse's writing, the digitalized version enables one to read it aloud—it facilitates the identification of the phonemes by compromising the graphic form of the writing (the graphemes). And according to Thévoz, phonemes and graphemes are equally critical in gaining an understanding of the text. They are "correspondent, making a system, and are mutually dependent, by reciprocal alibi…"[10]

For the purpose of reading Aloïse for content, for a sense of the structure of the text, or to appreciate the poetry inherent in the articulation of the words themselves, the transposed form is highly effective. As André Breton said, "thought forms itself in the mouth," and with Porret-Forel's facilitated access to Aloïse's thoughts articulated on page, one is enabled to fully and directly savor them—aloud.[11] To read Aloïse aloud, *en haut voix, en français*, is to experience her fully. Zarathustra and Aloïse were meant to be sung, and the transpositions prepare them for our mouths.

Aloïse's omission of punctuation, capitalization, and other phrase-delimiting techniques suggests that the torrent of images, words, and sounds filling the mind of the artist allowed no time for pause. Porret-Forel explains that Aloïse's texts follow a logic common in the Fourth Century, when

> *One was accustomed to reading aloud, so one finds chains of letters juxtaposed without punctuation or capitals…. Saint Augustine thought that the reading (at Catholic Mass) must be rendered present, that the scripta, written words, must become verba, words spoken to access existence. For him, the reader had to*

---

8   The translations are reprinted in Helvetica, the most internationally ubiquitous typeface. The documentary about Helvetica states that because of its omnipresence, the content naturally takes precedence over the form of the words.

9   For a discussion of Art Brut, see pages 207–211.

10   Thévoz, *Détournement*, 38.

11   "Aloud" implies the way one reads for pleasure, silently, but articulating the individual words internally. The inner narrative is a recital of the text as well.

literally breathe life into the text while filling the space
created of an animated language.[12]

Written to inform an oral reading, the task of infusing life into these liturgical texts involved intuiting inflection based on the content and the perceived form, rather than heeding the standard guides for proper parsing. The notion of *breathing life* into text incorporates the breath involved in speaking words; it accounts for the sounds formed in the mouth, pushed forth from the body, intonated. Quite literally, the words have passed from the page, through the lector, and are made audible by infusion with his breath.

The task of intuiting intonation is, in a way, central to that of translating Aloïse, and it is for this reason that Porret-Forel's transpositions can serve as a primer, conditioning the reader for the task of reading Aloïse's manuscripts. Aloïse's disregard for such formalities as punctuation and capitalization entails, for both transposer and translator, a difficult process of associating noun to verb or adjective, creating a cohesive image of which subjects correspond to which actions, and linking attributes properly. One must intuit from the context, rather than standard typographic markers, where one thought ends and another begins. One must suss out the sense within intermingling phrases, where thoughts don't end before another begins. And one must plot out those exquisite passages wherein a semantic-nesting-doll is born—a *jeu-de-mots* within the phrase, within the passage, within the page, within the fuller narrative of the written work.

* * *

In his essay "Strata or Historical Formations," Gilles Deleuze sums up all of perceivable reality as constituted of *words* and *things*, the articulable and the visible. The irreducible element of each is the utterance. The first utterance of a visibility, the "there is of light," happens in two parts: light shines and opens up a thing to seeing, and the light reflected by this thing is seen. The articulable, in contrast, begins with the statement, *there is*. That which is addressed in the form of a statement creates its own correlative object within the text (the object of the statement is particular to *that* statement), and the visible qualities

---

12   Porret-Forel, *Voleuse*, 59.

of an object evoke a visceral or sensual response. "The statement has primacy by virtue of the spontaneity of its conditions which give it a determining form ... It is because the articulable has primacy that the visible contests it with its own form."[13] In cases where the articulable element is pushed to the limits of what is potentially *sayable,* and the visible is pushed to the limits of what is *seeable,* where the limits of each property of a thing are exacerbated, one finds "the common limit that links one to the other, a limit with two irregular faces, a blind word and a mute vision."[14] Chez Aloïse, this limit is manifest as those exquisitely compossible states of legibility and tactility (in the original and transposed texts), and in the desire to nonetheless concomitantly consider the two intermingled forms.

The manuscript, the chirography of the author, manifests as ornate marks on paper when its density and illegibility produce an opacity of meaning. But this is not a matter of *decorating,* rather, it's evidence that the author meditated, or obsessed, over the visual articulation of each word. Here, one must read the text the way one reads a drawing—for the variation in line-width, pencil pressure, and grace in recording the hand's movement. What is *visible* is drawn form within the page, spatial composition, detailed articulation of drawn elements, and the relationship with other familiar pencil drawings.

Another form of "visibility" appears in decoding the scripted text, where what's "visible" is that which is most accessible—those signs, names, and places that offer ready associations to the reader (like "Napoleon," "the Magis," "the sphinx"). However the signs that appear easily available within Aloïse's text are complicated by their context. In context, we realize that these visible signs serve as sliding signifiers, and their meaning becomes opaque again. Thévoz notes that "the [Art Brut] artist takes a malign pleasure in provoking these phenomena of opacification of the sign which haunt the system of representation like its internal menace."[15] In recontextualizing signs, the artist attempts to redirect their association to signifiers, and thus re-assign the terms of their significance. In this reassignment of relationships between word

13   Gilles Deleuze, "Strata or Historical Formations: the Visible and the Articulable (Knowledge)," *Foucault* (Minneapolis: University of Minnesota Press, 1988), 67.
14   *Ibid.,* 65.
15   Thévoz, *Détournement,* 9.

and evoked image, the artist also tests the limits of *articulability*. She exhausts the limits of what can be said, or what image can be evoked with a sign specific to that text.

The process of establishing meaning through discovering associations within the body of Aloïse' text, through excavating the text from its scriptural opacity, is a delicate process. Each sign is specific to the passage in which it is written; to the body of text within which that passage is embedded; and to Aloïse's larger *œuvre*—its significance cannot simply be defined and then applied to each instance of its appearance. In Aloïse' writings, the interdependence of context-specific signs and their individual and metamorphosing meanings stretches the limits of the sayable, of what each word can articulate. And their calligraphic representations on paper, while hindering the accurate reading of each word, add an additional association to drawn form. The *Napoleon* of Aloïsian script is neither an illustration of Napoleon Bonaparte nor a direct association to the person himself. The calligraphic Napoleon, in its size, density, and overall figural accentuation exceeds the limits of written form. And because Aloïse makes myriad associations to Napoleon Bonaparte within her drawings, the Napoleon of her text exceeds the bounds of what one could say of him. Since Aloïse would write when her imagination couldn't see a form[16] (when the imagined found its most immediate corollary in word), and since images of Napoleon appear often in her drawings, the Napoleon of text (with all its filigree and serif) must be truly a unique entity.

In returning the textual transposition, in translation, to its original orientation on the page, my intent is not one of mimesis. Rather, I hope to acknowledge what is lost in linear, digital transcription of the text and to reinvest it with some of its original sensuality, some of its tactility. The reader must find the correct orientation for beginning the *lecture,* must locate where phrases begin and end, must discover the text as object for herself. This will require physically turning the book and plotting out the dialogue's continuation—handling the page as an object while reading is important in understanding the process

---

16   Aloïse said this when taking the Wartegg Symbol Test, which is a method of
       psychological evaluation employing drawing and drawing analysis. Its basis is
       similar to the Rorschach Test.

involved in its authoring. The inclusion of the original text in French serves as an illustration, so to speak, of the graphic quality forfeited in the typographic version.

Like Porret-Forel's transcription, which strips the text of its original body—of the materiality of the paper, of the figural scripting, and of the subtler elements like erasure and over-writing—the translation offered here is similarly voided of corporeality, though not without some consternation and the reluctant realization that such a task requires a lot of explanation. There are colloquialisms and archaic speech patterns that cannot be shoehorned into modern American English, and these nuances are in fact key to grasping the full effect of the text. This said, great pains have been taken to retain alliterations, rhymes, and homonymic *jeux-de-mots* where possible. As the transposition of manuscript loses much of its original vigor, the translation similarly sheds weight.

The intention here is to make Aloïse's texts accessible to English language readers, and the inclusion of the original may serve as reference for those who wish to consult both texts. The task of translation originated in my desire to better understand the original writing in French; it resulted in a fuller appreciation of its linguistic specificity, of all that is lost in translation. *"Le contexte est réducteur de sens, dit-on..."*[17] In reading Aloïse it is helpful to possess equally vast knowledge of opera, poetry, European history and its personages and places, Swiss/French/German folk songs and folklore, the Bible, and alchemy. Assuming that most readers don't, a partial lexicon is included with this text. While it's useful as a point of departure for beginning to understand the multitude of references and the narratives woven together, the terms must only be read as an incomplete guide. These are simply landmark terms, and the body of the text exists in the *inframince*. The fluid in-between poetry is left open to mis/interpretation.

Circumnavigating a textual firmament spangled with malapropisms, neologisms, and deadly serious plays on words requires an informed, yet personal discovery of the text. For many Art Brut authors and artists, the opacification of meaning is a natural occurrence. In some cases the author intends to be opaque, as a means of securing privacy

---

17   "Context is a reducer of meaning, they say." Thévoz, *Détournement*, 38.

and preventing communication to subsequent readers. In other cases, as obsession with obscuring the text's sense results in an utter neglect for the content, the text becomes a field of hieroglyphics, nonspecific meaning, or insignificant signifiers. In the case of Aloïse, the text is simply super-subjective: the codification of the terms, the scripting, and the multitude of possible meanings can only be truly understood by their author. This said, one ought to hazard informed guesses as to the intended sense, with the understanding that within the *multi-torte*[18] of Aloïsian linguistics there is not one correct reading to be gleaned.

Perhaps the best one can hope for is a tragic reading—for Roland Barthes, this is one in which the reader allows the double and triple entendres to open onto a complete understanding of the full implications of the text and from here deduces a sense of it. This is not to say that the full sense of the text will then be transparent. Rather, such a reading will reveal a web of signifiers flush with meaning, one that vibrates for its fluidity, and affords linguistic potentialities otherwise impossible. *Tragedy* in this sense includes the reader, the spectator, as a possible character in the Aloïsian universe. The likelihood for misunderstanding is exhilaratingly imminent and provocative of further investigation.

---

18   "Multi-torte" is an Aloïsian neologism meaning multi-layered cake.

LETTRE À GUILLAUME II
28 avril 1917

Lausanne ce 28-IV-1917

Lors de mon court séjour à Berlin, je me suis fa-
miliarisée avec la simplicité d'un empereur
dont le trône m'écraserait s'il n'était pieux.
J'en appelle donc à sa condescendance pour lui
communiquer franchement ma pensée ainsi
qu'à un cher confesseur et protecteur de la Suisse.
Certaine que la guerre nous a été épargnée
grâce à Dieu par l'intermédiaire de votre impériale bonté, je ne peux m'empêcher de
vous exprimer avec ardeur, une joie inti-
me et délirante de rescapée, ma profonde gratitude. Je vais vous confier tout d'abord
un grand souci qui me touche de près :
Pour parer à une épidémie de sans-travails
sans cesse grandissante, Monsieur de Coppet,
ex-président de la Confédération Suisse, a résolu
de créer des industries nouvelles pour occu-
per les hommes de n'importe quelle natio-
nalité chez vous. Le maintien momentané
des ateliers d'uniformes militaires qui doivent se fermer à la fin de mai, en se char-
geant peut-être à l'avenir des écoulements
de sociétés subventionnées par l'état, entre
d'assister les femmes dans la misère.
Permettez que je recommande à votre haute
influence, Monsieur de Coppet, persuadée

que vous pourrez d'un mot aplanir les difficultés qu'il rencontrera, manquant totalement de matières premières ⬛⬛⬛ Majesté de toute mon âme depuis que m'incombe cette lourde et épouvantable responsabilité de la guerre mondiale. Supposant que vous avez été contraint à la déclarer par l'incrédulité générale, j'ai jeté à tous les vents votre ancien titre d'empereur de paix. Vous serez probablement considéré et fanatiquement aimé, comme tel.

En qualité d'antimilitariste je cherche en vain à établir la paix sans que la majorité des humains soient chrétiens. En admettant le travail de la nature en esprit, la guerre demeure en esprit. La splendide et parfaite harmonie de la nature, produite par le soleil provenant du centre vital de la terre [je ne vois qu'une planète quoi qu'en disent les astronomes, une seule pomme de l'amour divin] dans la cohésion de facteurs opposés; laisse entrevoir le Saint-Esprit unissant le bien au mal pour obtenir la lumière ou amour divin qui fusionne harmonieusement les races, les nations et les religions dans la paix de Dieu qui surpasse toute intelligence. Le premier symbole de l'amour divin est le don de la nature créée par le grand horloger disait Voltaire. Le deuxième symbole est le don du Christ, Dieu manifesté en chair. Il est le chemin, la vérité et la vie: Il nous montre le chemin au moyen des paraboles mises en pratique au propre et au figuré / spirituellement et matériellement / sur terre. La vérité dans le sacrifice mutuel ainsi la plante à l'embryon; la nouvelle naissance à la vertu afin d'obtenir la terre promise sur terre à la paix. La vie dans la foi en un Dieu d'amour, tout-puissant, défenseur du droit et de la justice sur terre. Je suis étonné avec l'amour divin.

Tout est bien qui finit bien

La vie éternelle dans la résurrection de l'âme dans le corps de nos bien-aimés abandonnés sur terre; en sorte que la vie éternelle est transmise de génération en génération sur terre...... Une paix durable n'aurait pu être établie sans l'anéantissement des temples d'or, bien sordide et vermeil, piédestal de l'égoïsme humain criminel, idole que l'on a adorée au lieu et place du Créateur-Sauveur-Rédempteur. Par conséquent devant l'écroulement des grandeurs terrestres, nous sommes obligés pour être heureux, de revenir à une vie chrétienne, étant soumis, en athée aussi, aux lois divines, immuables d'après lesquelles on récolte indubitablement ce qu'on sème.

Au cas où vous aimeriez la misère en lambeaux
Vous seriez inévitablement des flambeaux
Le troisième symbole de l'amour divin c'est
la paix et ceux qui la procurent souvent
au prix de leur vie entière ou de leur sang,
pour l'enfanter il faut se sacrifier avec a-
mour / Bientôt plus de paix . G.I parle de paix .

Tableau qui illumine   Une inspiration divine
Dès votre enfance   De la reconnaissance,
Au Christ Sauveur   Dont le sacré cœur.
Par son sacrifice féconde   L'âme du monde

Pourquoi donc en évoquant votre souvenir
est-ce que je vibre comme une cloche an-
nonçant des épousailles d'anges ? mou-
rant lentement d'un amour ineffable
que me suggère votre regard splendide
rencontré par hasard à la revue de Pots-
dam 1913 . Vous étiez étincelant des pieds
à la tête, divinisé par le rayonnement sublime de votre cher visage .

Ma paupière doucement se baisse,
Votre regard éblouissant laisse,
Une empreinte noble et sacrée,
Profonde pure et azurée
Dans mon pauvre cœur .
La majestueuse douceur
Ma scelle l'âme,? la vie .
Oh ! mon Dieu j'en suis ravie . /.

L'impulsion de cet enchantement m'agenouille dévotement derrière la porte où vous aviez disparu.

Ô douleur! Ô désespoir! je ne parviens pas à saisir les fleurs délicates aux pénétrants parfums que vous aviez involontairement déposées dans chaque repli de mon cœur emmuré par la misère. Que ne puis-je retremper mon âme en feu, dans les feux de firmament constellé d'étoiles d'un homme inaccessible que j'aime éperdument! Seul un miracle de l'amour divin peut raser les murs qui m'en séparent éternellement. Effondrée, baisant les dalles froides devant l'autel du Seigneur Jésus, je supplie d'intercéder auprès de Dieu le Père, avec actions de grâces, afin qu'il éloigne tout danger qui vous menace. Dans le parc de Sans-Souci, toujours et encore une adorable apparition féminine me suit et m'enveloppe délicieusement de son merveilleux sourire (tel une brise printanière) qui m'a guérie de la nostalgie. Je la vois en rêve en aigle-colombe planer idéalement rose en Impératrice de paix d'Allemagne

29

sur la tête précieuse de la Majesté l'empereur de paix Wilhelm II.

Le ciel et la terre passeront,
mais mes paroles ne passeront.

Mathieu 24.55

Chercher mon âme dans vos grands yeux
Où se mire le firmament constellé d'étoiles des cieux,
Reposer, un instant au moins mon regard mouillé
Sur ce visage aux traits réguliers empreints de majesté
Surprenante et adorable
~~Merveilleuse~~ apparition fictive
Ainsi la rend languissante et pensive,
Ce nuage ~~blanc~~ bleu et rose
Baise doucement la terre morose,
Te réflétant l'immensité des mers
Vil des entrailles purgées des enfers
L'écueil par le flot frémissant caressé
Fouille le nuage vermeil échevelé .
Entoure avec ~~douceur~~ la porte des ciel
Efface l'amertume du fiel
— Ô nature miraculeuse, divine école
Incarne toi, donne moi ton obole !
— Ô ~~Christ que je veilles ou non malgré toi~~
Dans la souffrance ~~donne à Dieu ton âme~~
Dit le Tout-Puissant, ~~Rédempteur~~
Mon amour t'envoit le Christ Rédempteur

LETTER TO GUILLAUME II
28 April 1917

Lausanne   ce 28 IV 1917

Majesty !

During my short stay in Berlin I became fa-
miliarized with the simplicity of an emperor
whose throne would crush me if he were not pious.
I appeal therefore to his condescendence to
communicate frankly to him my thoughts as if
to a dear confessor and protector of Switzerland
Certain that the war has been spared from us
thank God by the intermediary of your imperial bounty, I cannot prevent myself from
expressing to you with ardor an intimate and del-
irious joy of survivor my profound gratitude. I will confide to you straight away
a great concern that touches me closely:
To ward off an epidemic of without-works
endlessly growing Monsieur de Coppet
ex president of the Swiss Confederation, has resolved
to create new industries to occupy
the   men   of   any   nation-
ality here at home. The momentary maintenance
of the military uniform ateliers which must close at the end of May, while taking
care perhaps in the future, of state subsidized
equipment societies by the state, in view
of assisting the impoverished women
Permit that I recommend to your high
influence Monsieur de Coppet, persuaded

that you could with a word smooth out the difficulties
that he will encounter, lacking totally in
raw material   Majesty of all
my soul since he obliged to this heavy
and dreadful responsibility of the world
war. Supposing that you had been con-
strained to declare it by the general incredulity,
I threw to all the winds your old title of emperor of peace. You will be probably considered
and fanatically loved, like this.
In antimilitarist capacity I search in vain
to establish peace without the majority of
humans being Christian. In admitting the
work of nature in spirit, the war remains in spirit. The splendid and perfect
harmony of nature, produced by the sun
arisen from the vital center of the earth [I see
but one planet regardless of what the astro-
nomers say, a solitary divine love apple]
in the cohesion of opposing factors; allow a
glimpse of the Saint-Esprit unifying the good and
evil to obtain the light or divine love
which   harmoniously fuses   the
races, the nations and the religions in the
peace of God who surpasses all intelligence.
The first symbol of divine love is the
gift of nature created by the great Clockmaker

said Voltaire. The second symbol is the gift
of the Christ, God manifested in flesh. He is the path, the truth and the life: He shows us the path by way of parables put in prac-
tice literally and figuratively spiritually and
materially on earth. The truth in
the mutual sacrifice thus the plant within the embr
yo; the new birth to virtue in order to obtain the promised land on earth "peace"
The life in the faith in a God of love, all-
powerful, defender of the right and the justice on
earth. I am amazed by the divine love.
            All   is   well   that ends well
The eternal life in the resurrection of the soul
in the body of our beloved   abandoned
on earth; so that the   eternal   life   is
transmitted from generation to generation
on earth.. An enduring peace could not
have been established without the destruction
of the golden temples, quite sordid and vermillion, ped-
estals of the human criminal egotism, idols
adored in place of the Creator-
Savior - Redeemer. Consequently   before the collapsing of the terrestrial grandeurs
   we   are   forced in order to be happy,
to return to a Christian life, being sub-
jected, in atheism too, to the divine laws, immut-
able according to those in which one harvests indubitab

bly that which one sows
In case you would love tattered misery
You would inevitably be beacons
The third symbol of divine love is
peace and those who procure it often
at the price of their entire life or of their blood,
for to birth it it is necessary to sacrifice oneself with l-
ove, Very soon more Peace. G.II speak of Peace.
Tableau that illuminates A divine inspiration
Since our infancy Of the reconnaissance,
Tothe Christ Savior the sacred heart of whom.
By his fecund sacrifice seeds The soul of the world

Why then in evoking your memory
is it that I vibrate like a bell an-
nouncing the nuptials of angels? dying slowly of an ineffable love
suggested to me by your splendid gaze
encountered by chance at the revue of Pots-
dam 1913. You were shimmering from head
to foot, deified by the sublime radi-
ance of your dear face.

My eyelid modestly lowers,
Your regard stunningly lingers,
An imprint noble and sacred,
Profound pure and azure
In my poor heart.
His majestic softness
Seals up my soul for Life.
Oh! my god I am in rapture./.

The impulsion of this enchantment brings me to my knees devotedly behind the door where you disappeared.

Ô sorrow! Ô dispair! I never managed to seize the delicate flowers and their penetrating perfumes that you were involuntarily depositing in each corner of my heart immured by misery That can I not requench my blazing soul, in the eyes of star-studded firmament of an inaccessible man whom I love passionately! Only a miracle of the divine love can raze the walls that have eternally separated me from him. Prostrate, kissing the cold flagstones before the altar of the Savvior Jesus I implore him to intercede to God the Father ! with actions of grace, in order to ward off all danger that would threaten you.

        In the park of Sans Souci, always and ever more an adorable female apparition follows me and envelopes me deliciously in her marvellous smile (such a spring breeze) which cured me of nostalgia! I see her in a dream as an eagle-dove soaring ideally rose as of Empress of peace of Germany on the precious head of his Majesty the em-

peror   of   Peace   Wilhelm   II .

Heaven and earth will pass,
But my words will not pass.

Matthew 24.35

To search for my soul in your great eyes
That mirror the star-studded firmament of the skies
To rest, an instant at least, my tearful visage,
On this fine-featured majesty imprinted face.
Astonishing and adorable

fictive   apparition

Which renders her languid and pensive,

This cloud variegated white blue and rose

Softly   kisses the morose   earth,

Reflecting to you the immensity of the seas

Sees its entrails purged of the damnation

The reef by the quivering tide caressed

Search the vermillion tousled cloud

delicious
Set ajar with ravishment the door of the heavens
slowly
Efface the bitterness of rancor

-Ô miraculous nature, divine   school

Incarnate yourself, give me your contribution!

that you want it or not in spite of yourself
-Ô man that   you want it or not
your soul belongs to me
In suffering give God his name
Savior
Says the All-Powerful Redem
My love sends you the Christ Redeemer

LA GRANDE MADONNE À VALLOTTON

25 mars 1920

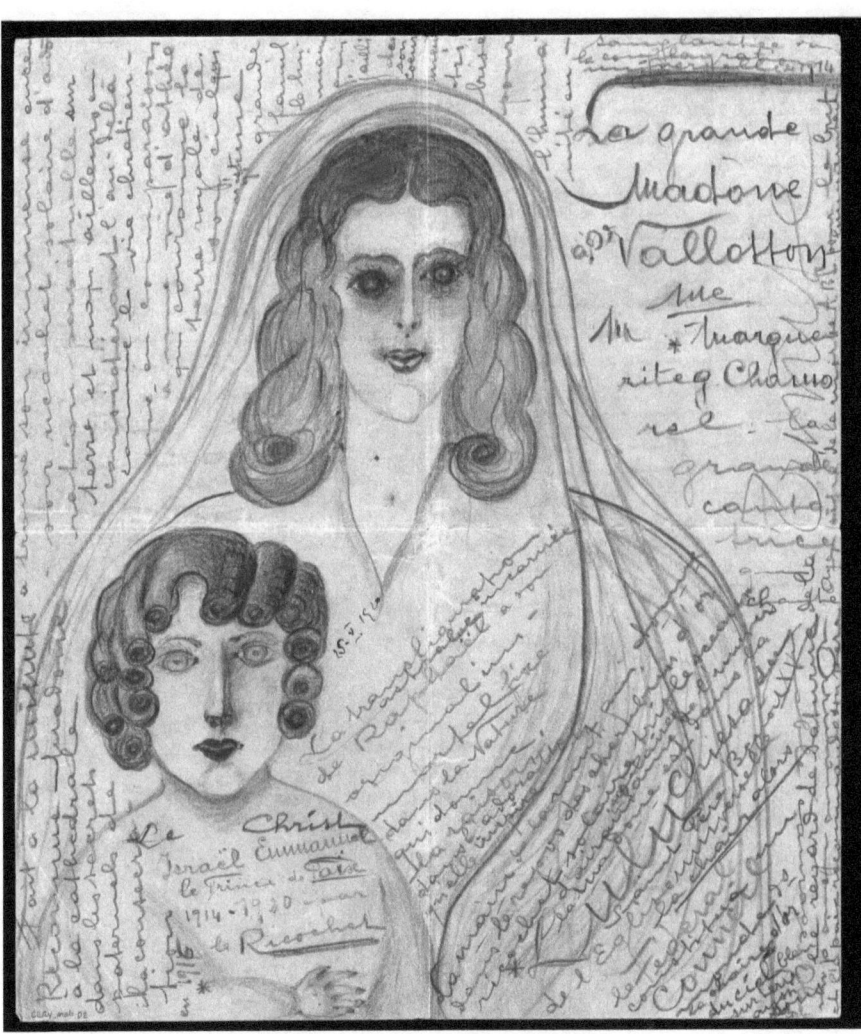

41

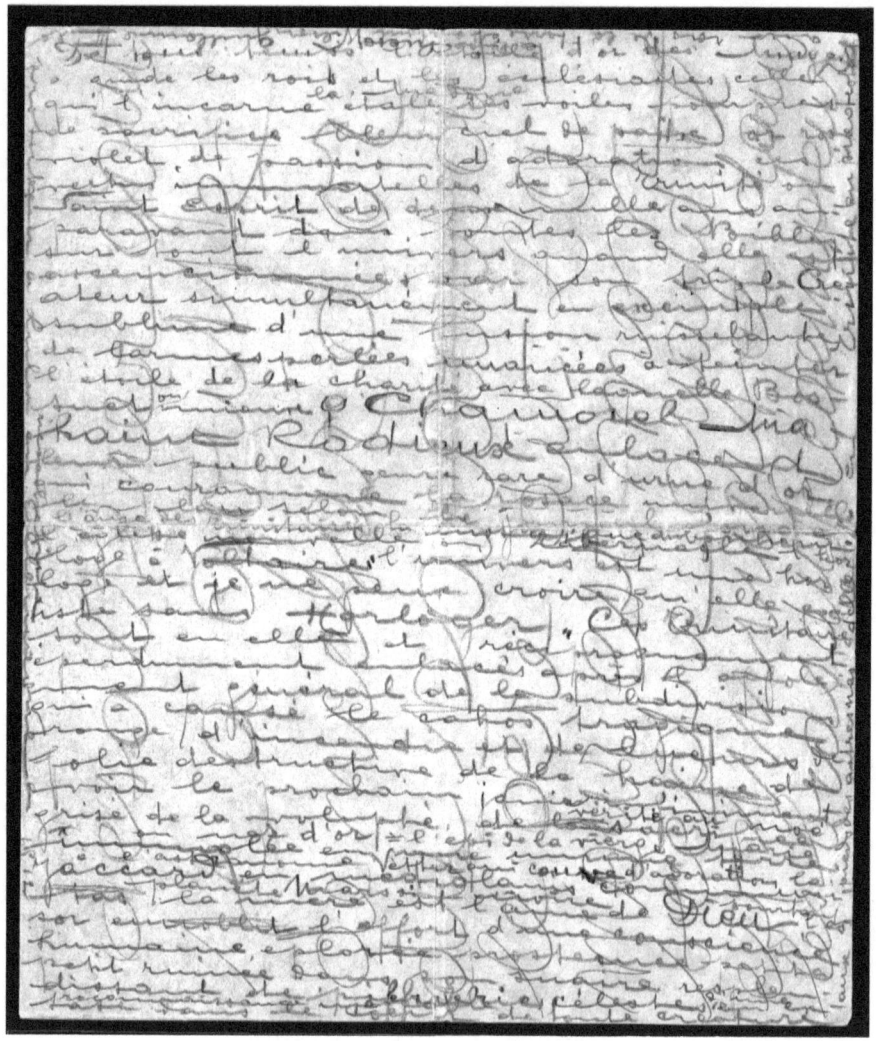

THE GREAT MADONNA OF VALLOTTON

25 March 1920

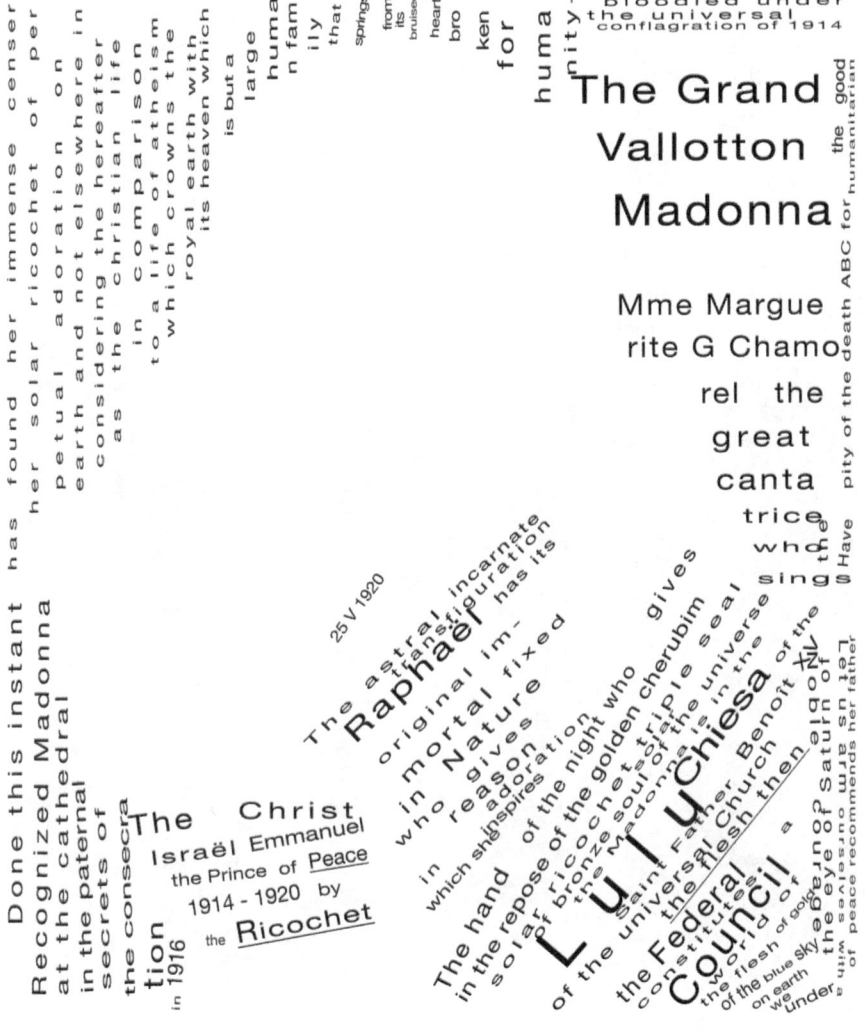

Done this instant has found her immense censer
Recognized Madonna her solar ricochet of per
at the cathedral petual adoration on
in the paternal earth and not elsewhere in
secrets of considering the hereafter
the consecra as the christian life
tion in comparison
in 1916 to a life of atheism
which crowns the
royal earth with
its heaven which
is but a
large
huma
n fam
ily
that
springs
from
its
bruised
heart
bro
ken
for
huma
nity-

bloodied under
the universal
conflagration of 1914

The Grand

Vallotton

Madonna

Mme Margue
rite G Chamo
rel   the
great
canta
trice
who
sings

good
the
death ABC for humanitarian
pity of the death
Have

25 V 1920

The astral incarnate
transfiguration
Raphaël has its
original im-
mortal fixed
in Nature
who gives
reason
in
adoration
which she inspires

The   Christ
Israël Emmanuel
the Prince of Peace
1914 - 1920 by
the Ricochet

The hand of the golden cherubim who gives
in the repose of the night who gives
of bronze soul of the universe
solar ricochet triple seal
Lu u Chiesa
of the universal church
Saint Father Benoît
the flesh of the
the Federal
Council
constitutes a
the flesh of gold world of
of the blue sky eye of saturn
on earth
under
of peace recommends her father

At all times the golden star of the Magi
has guided the kings and the ecclesiasts the one
the Madonna
who incarnates it exposes her sacrificial crimson
veils of sky blue peace gold rose
violet of passion of adoration these
immortal virtues of the Trinity or
Saint Esprit of two thousand years previously in all the Bibles
in all the universe when she is
simultaneously ascensioned
by her triple Creator as sublime
example of a streaming fusion
of pearled nuanced tears for to tinge
the star of charity with which Bos-
suet or better gChamorel Mahaim Rodieux intertwine
their public rare kind of golden urn
that crowns the universal rosette
the ... according to the ... the mosaic
the soul of the Universal Church
clock of Voltaire: the universe is a clock and I can not believe that it exists without a clockmaker. These Trinitaries
are within her and reciprocally
headlessly intertwined after the general
panic of the subdivision
that caused the tragic red
chaos of flies and of glows or
destructive folly of hate to
see the next day infinitely arise
ashen from the voluptuousness of truth
immolated as a sacrifice Mary
golden nose / = bristle of the virgin
of the astronomer Vetter who covers in adoration the unique earth
Jaccard in
planet Mars so black and yet
the mother is the soul of God
development enobles the effort of a human
conscience tearful grovelling little by
little ruined in her resplendent
shroud of celestial precious stones as
recognition of in the heart of every creature

(superimposed large lettering) to quench at last as the father says where my immortal Royal ascent the arms of the Redeemer

the protector of Lulu in Germany in 1912

pedestal Trinity in at the ... feet of the stars born of her

LE NOËL DE SAINT-ROSAIRE

c. 1921

Le Noël de Saint-Rosaire-
Mahaim mon chare
bonté volé à vendre
Recteur de l'université!

qu'on applique sur une pierre noire dans le ciel
de la nuit suivant la sente du serac géant
dans une fleur morte. Plus fait lire un feuil-
let tombé de la tempête morale l'aveugle en
qui montrant un arbre obscur qui doit fleurir
en apothéose de tour de Babel sans la
parole de Dieu qui a été faite chair dans
la mappemonde sur l'Évangile de l'Esplanier
incarné avec son Christ en croix de contrefaç-
ialité en collaboration de création de Saint Hérédit-
intaires trois michel-ange triple beauté d'airain des mille
temples au plafond d'or métal de rosace de palmes en une couronne immarcessible astrale
de la châsse plus dans l'orage dans la nuit
sous la lune éclipse phénomènes quotidiens font
transparaître en paléographie dans les temples
des jardins des dieux d'Amérique remarquable
des très hautes murailles de la Jérusalem d'or qui
surplombe les nouveaux cieux la nouvelle terre
de la fleur de soufre douleur des volcans
teint en fleurissant les pierres précieuses saphir

hyacinthe = bleu foncé le jacinthe la soeriesmaudet — les sont
blindées d'or jouent le role de Psyche prisme dans la
dilatation du fer forgé surchauffé des cratères
résiste en aimants tissus moléculaire prennent
lumineux en amphithéâtre 12 mille camp de la
Jérusalem nouvelle biblique superposés qui elles composent
la conformation des montagnes de l'Himalaya
dessinent en radium céleste les contours de la terre
dans le tonnerre comme le nom l'indique 12 mille
tours étoiles en mots ou concours représentent les cours des
ciels des temples au plafond d'or et pur formes de Tour Eiffel en
rosaces de la cathédrale de Reims de 1440 ou bien 12 mille lobes plans
des montagnes rocheuses volcaniques en contour
asiatique comme toutes les chaînes de l'océan glacial
arctique des deux pôles forment l'enveloppe universelle de la terre étoilé dans la mappemonde en
voit du monde en amphithéon de domino de croisade
superposés des Cordillères et du l'aurisantkar en couronne
de boistir d'or de Félix Faure a ajouté à ses croisade à l'incarné ou Wilson
avec ses soldats aux sentiments de croates dont les cœurs sont à
la Suisse reconnaît l'âge d'or en simonie sur le pays
bleu ou le ciel bleu la Sinose qui a fait de son cratère éteint
une autel Dieu depuis les trois collines de Lausanne la Jérusa-
lème pierres angulaires précieuses dans des cieux de Christ phrases
dans l'éclair toujours en français clichés universels en étoile
les tragédien géant 21 tolérance chrétienne en un Pocalepet
12 mille cratères dans soit de mille ans. Paix inter na-
tionna a dit Wilson le 15 novembre reconnaît les volcanisé
autres terme pas ou pas de géant de Haute cour d'ar-
bitrage céleste supérieure à ses foyers terrestre de matière
en fusion de sociétés universelles de différents corps
fédérations en couleurs de l'arc en ciel à Vallotton Paul préaplein international
autrefois abondamment comorme 20 ans prédicateur des foules
de Paris avec les 4 Bridel et Saillens qui ont annoncé l'impératrice de Paris
un grand Kaiser correspondent à décoration comme laissochet
à vie en revanche de sa médaille impériale de la Madona Raphaël
lors de la fondation de l'Église universelle en 1917
le Pacificateur à corps et palme d'or costume il endosse à l'école impériale de créa
et l'université sont responsables de la construction de la ville
Sainte en connaissance tenant de phares, horloge à Besnard et
celle à Voltaire de tabernacle des cieux du ciel dans l'univers
fils de Balthasar en réformateur de la Suisse soui volupté des
mappemonde fenêtre souci sur Voltaire de Ferney sur le ricochet entre ciel
commence et le pasteur Herrick le parlent d'Auguste Wilhelm le Kronprinz
de Dryander allocution en place ostinium Camille Flammarion
Il doivent expliquer cette fleur du tournesol dix volcan du ciel

NOËL OF SAINT-ROSAIRE

c. 1921

The Noël of Saint-Rosaire-
Mahaim my guiding light
of kindness stolen to return to
rector of the University !

Albert 1921

Mahaim

proftheologist

decorated

psychoanalyst

Couldn't one send back these telepathists who kill me by writing Müller so loved the world he saves

must live in Walter Scott with his son
the doctor Fritz Heim trinitary prof
as an immortal

that one applies to a black earth in the veils
by the rivals without foreign
of the night following the incline of the giant glacier
situations
in a dead flower makes him read a page
fallen from the moral tempest the blind in
showing him a dark tree which must flower
in apotheosis of the Tower of Babel without the
word of God which has been made flesh in
the world-map that the Evangel of Eplattenier
incarnated with his Christ on the cross of consubstan
tiality in collaboration from creation of Saint Father Tri
nitaries three Michel Angel triple bronze seal of the 12 thousand
The throne the science is narrow without the
temples with gold metal ceilings of rosettes of pal-
three nests of the Infinite Chamorel Mahaim Kaiser
ms in an imperishable astral crown
Wilhelm II Very High who went to holy war in 1912
of the charity fuses in the tumult in the night
under the eclipsed moon quotidien phenomena are made to
transpire in paleography in the temples
and the Chinese
of the gardens of the gods of America (remarkable example
of the very high murals of the golden Jerusalem which
overhangs the new heavens the new earth
ingredient
of the sulfer flower-sorrow   [gold sdar]of the extinguished
volcanoes flowering precious stones sapphire

The tiara of Leon XIII 1920 a cross surmounted by the mountain chains the kiss his noble footprints that once stormed to Gimel carried in triumph

Mantegna

theologist Mahaim on his path of his army corps that did not manage to have seen but half time over

53

talmud=dark blue the hyacinth the poerlesmaiden--all are
reinforced with gold playing the role of psyche prism in the
dilation of the overheated forged iron of the craters
resists in cement molecular tissues stones
luminous in amphitheater 12 thousand calculations from the
biblical New Jerusalem superimposed that they compose
the configuration of the mountains of the Himalayas
draw in celestial radii the contours of the earth
in the commotion as the name indicates 12 thousand stages
towers stars in wedding celebrations or competition represent the course of the
bases as an immense earthly square-star following the lanes and straits of the
heavens of the temples with a ceiling of pure gold formed of Eiffel Towers in
rosettes of the cathedral of Reims of 144 or well 12 thousand foiled surfaces
of rocky volcanic mountains in contour
asiatic like all the chains of the glacial arctic
ocean of both poles form the universal envelope of the earth star in the worldmap as
a roof of the world as domino amphitrion of superimposed
crusades from the Cordileras and from the Gaurisankar (as crown)
of the golden fleeces of Felix Faure added to his crusade at the incarnation or Wilson
with his soldiers of sentiments of crusaders whose hearts go to
Switzerland recognize the golden age as synonym for the blue
country or the blue sky Switzerland who made of his extinguished crater
an altar-God since the three hills of Lausanne the Jerusalem of angular precious stones canopy of the climes of chrysophrase
in the flash always in French universal clichés in stars
in form of fabric Pénélope terrestrial envelope
of the Magi in gamut of 24 volcanoes subdivided in a Topocatepelt
of 12 thousand craters the peace of a thousand years.Pax inter na-
tiones said Wilson the 15 November 1921 recover these volcanoes in
other words pax or giant steps of High court of celestial
superior arbitration to these terrestrial foyers of materials
in fusion of universal societies of different corpo-
rations in colors of the rainbow to Vallotton Paul formerly international
preceptor abundantly crowned 20 years predicator of the crowds
in Paris with the 4 Bridel and Saillens who announced the empress of Peace
of the grand Kaiser corresponding to decoration like the ricochet
to life nevertheless of his imperial medal of the Raphaelite Madonna wearing a tiara
recognized at the time of the founding of the universal church in 1917 which one
gives by the Pacificator in the press cup and golden palm pompous
costume that he endorses at the imperial school of creation
of the university are responsibles for the construction of the holy
city in reminiscence as many lighthouses Besnard clocks and
that of Voltaire of tabernacle the key of the heavens in the burning of Balthasar in reformation of Switzerland [worry] thief of
world-map flower of worry by Voltaire of Ferney by the ricochet Lulu here
as with the pastor Henninke pastor of Auguste Wilhelm the Kronprinz-
substitute of vacationing Dryander post obtained by Camille Delessert
in 1912 They must apply this flower of the forum of the volcano of the heavens
this world map of sans Souci seen in Switzerland before Cesar on the black

grandiose work of Wilson by the 1914 of integration contour universal of the earth at the earth

that consists in emphasizing the tower of Babel in dedicating a religion to his God which he is studying the laws from the heavens of the summary. Of marbel of crystal of gold subsists in temple of golden ceiling. To Abraham Lincoln For the Evangel. For the Kings. Chamorel. overhangs the rocks that she envelopes. and a consort.

ÉCRIT SUR UNE FEUILLE DE PAPIER D'ARGENT

1924–1942

de le manteau de toi — en
"seguido Napol." en
visite à Pregny en Pie X
et Paderewsky — palace
exposition des sphinx
de Rumine le reblan-
chir! la lunette — Chamo-
nal n'a fait lanterna
à pergola rose (lustre) d'Ouchy
le sacre de Napoléon —
en lampe éternel amour
le monde a ses pieds —
avec les porta et sa le
Coppet sa rose à la main —
1er et brodequin de Thali-
tous ces musiciens amou-
que la terre et leurs ballets la
valse bleue de la Corse et pri-
mario presous les arceaux
fleuris dans les défilés de Co-
so fleuris, l'émulation
de le char à la Cérès = O coloy
le immoligé sur l'autel sur
le bau de Hygie la botte du
13 ou Enfant et Carousel

WRITING ON SILVER PAPER
1924–1942

in the ball manteau
"Eseguirlo Napoli

visiting Pregny as Pie X

and Paderewsky palace
exhibition of the sphinxes
of Rumine to whitewash
it : the telescope of Chamorel has kept us waiting
calendered
in rose pergola d'Ouchy
the coronation of Napoleon
in eternal love   lamp
a   world at his   feet
with some pasta and his de
Coppet his rose in   hand
in the brodequin of Thalie
All these musicians crown
the earth and their ballets the
pretty
blue waltz of Corsica and its
marriages under the flowered
arches in the processions of rib
boned parade floats
in the float of Ceres = ô dove
immolated on the altar of
the ban of Lygie the hood of the
Bon Enfant and the Carousel

À MADEMOISELLE ROSINE
après 1942

Ô Mademoiselle Rosine
Vous êtes grande en tout comme les
blés en mai - Et votre main n'est
pas plus large qu'une rose - Pour vos
pied ma chère enfant c'est autre...
Le prince qui épousa Cendrillon l'eut
aimé - Comme artiste le
geste est beau de ton forme Et vous
chantez comment dirai-je ? en
virtuose - Et vous avez déjà bien a-
vant d'être éclose. Un petit goût à vous
piquant et parfumé. Je sais que
vous avez dix ans Mademoiselle
Et que vous êtes grande et qu'il faut
qu'on cisèle ses vers - Si vous allez
par les trouvez bons ? Vous êtes
mon bébé quasiment ma femme
acceptez mon hommage et recevez
Madame sans rougir du présent
ce ... d'étudiant... de la fortune de bonbons
par albert mérat ....
Il est une chanson d'amour de Naples
le soleil brille sur tous les amoureux d'...
Naples où les amants prêtent toujours ser-
ment de mariage - des amis de noce
en voyage d'Orient : dans les falaises

fleurs d'oranger ne quittez pas mes
bras dans les ballets de la fête d'Ortigosa
Peuple français vous êtes des braves
quand la France ouvre ses bras
les phares de feu de l'île de Croix
ou l'île de Ray mes d'oreille comme une étoile claire au front de
la France — vous amphore
ou rouge pêcheurs la Sirène,
Liberté qui refleurira quand
elle ouvre ses bras son cor-
set d'or et son manteau royal
à agenouiller Victoria Hall dedans
son auditoire militaire, d'autre
strophes de chant de l'an nouveau du Bon-Enfant et ses cadeaux le la pêche imaculeuse
le sceptre et le brodequins de Thalie
tout fleurit sous le sceptre fleuri
de Bonaparte et son manteau de cuivre
à propriété pia de Saint Pierre
de fleurs de fruits de la nature de
grenadille bleue de Sans-Souci
ou de la couronne impériale de la
Salle des orchidées rose, du mariage
de Gaule peintre à Paris ou
cour de Preguy (Schenk et roi)

la Rosia..... Prières pour la Bretagne - l'épouse du Barde.
la prière des matelots = genoise.
Prédications qui faisant fleurir
la colonne de Juillet s'illuminait de bouquet final de Bengale
de fête et dancing Vénitiennes, de gondoles fleuries en lanternes de Venise d'or
de Jean-Pierre Cailloc'h = qu'il fut président
Lebrun et sa loggia théâtrale soldat -
sa reine est venue - ancien marinier français et poète breton -
sa femme Lecoire à Montbenon
à Lausanne gigantesque volant
de pourpre de soie fleuris des étudiants. couronnement des bannières elle avait l'air d'être portée en triomphe la France quand
le chef d'orchestre après son Solo Seigneur Dieu
d'opéra ? lui présentait une
gerbe lys à genoux relevait sa longue
traîne de la reine dans son
Carosse (en couronne américaines à Paris à l'instar des reines
de beauté des ballets des dames aux
Camélias) on aussi la revêtue
en apothéose d'un manteau de héraldique
pourpra qui couvre de gloire la Suisse

française · /. Chez les Papes à A-
vignon — Orange et Nice
la terre royales est son ouvrage fleur
lancée dans l'espace en
batailles de fleurs et chante
le soleil le ciel de lit et
et la Onregtano de la mer en
en grande tenue - dans les printemps
vif très éclatant - le no
sous son dais bleu elle s'endort
mille fleurs
Marsih qui incantatrices met-
tait des pi dans une bottelsha-
ped des anglais à tous ses
auditoires — — — — je le re Ile
commande à Dieu l'orange
ne restait pas comme un
Cyprès sur le tombeau d'l'humanité sans les fêtes théâtrales
en mariage des épées au-dessus d'elles
d'un écrin d'un diadème de perles
de diamants. On sent le lion
dans l'ombre qui construi-
sit l'Achilléion de Corfou d'elle,
Christonamos lui parlant grec
bras dessus bras dessous
euse Vollebourquine ! Toten velled
zaziett aug yalann dans le talon
commande à Dieu cher ange Élisabeth

d'achille" ou dans un navire dal Sol

on sent le croyait à l'ombre Vivante. Sépia-
tomberait sur lui dans l'écriture d'Éros
de la Guintebrose de l'atelier Rubens
peintre hollandais de Bichonnant—
sement et passionnément à vos cô-
tés dans polyphonie pastorale enla
née en rose d'armide au château
de Montaulieu (de Beaulieu) Rosa
lie de la Chablière en peinture
sur votre table du soleil au jardin
de Beau-Soleil impassionnait du
prof. Bernardin de Saint Pierre — on
baisant le manteau monacal de
la Falda de Pie XI de Roméo et
Juliette château en gondole fleurie ou
à genoux le roi de Naples au
pieds de Zita d° les balcons d'amou-
diers — magnoliers ou d'abricotiers
de cerisiers — pêchers colliers et boucles d'oreilles qui ne coûtait qu'un
baiser. et la chanson: ses deux bras
lui servait d'échelle pour monter (sur les orgues) sur le cerisier
d'où je souriais à la belle qui
me tendais son tablier et de ses
fruits pourpres et vermeils je lui

faisais pour l'amuser des colliers, des
boucles d'oreilles qui ne coûtaient
qu'un baiser. Le printemps en fleurs
premières brises soufflent dans la
plaine et sur les côteaux. Il faut aller
voir mûrir les cerises pour les amoureux et pour les oiseaux..... j'avais
deux ans de plus que Rose peu
d'esprit elle l'avait tout je savais
bien une chose c'était de l'aimer
beaucoup. la voir l'adorer le lui
dire était le refrain de mon coeur
dans son regard dans son pouvoir
je voyais naître mon bonheur.
————— Pour te fêter maman
chérie j'ai mis ma robe fleurie
sur le manteau à l'île des Pans
était peint le printemps. Sur
mon visage le plus joli sourire
j'ai mis mon ruban le plus coquet
en présentant mes hommages
une grenadille bleue à la main.
toute sorte de bouquets ———
My darling a butterfly bouquet
a rose over your corall lips —
for their flus la ad'ring - diamond
en couronnes de la terre royale

le soir immense;
en baise main de la Walewska à
l'inkenstein et les bras en collier
d'elle sur Napoléon étendu sur le
canapé - - - - - il déchire les guir-
lande de rose. Obermwald déchire
les voiles épanchement sen-
timentaux au tableau idyl-
lique - Le soleil parle à la terre et lui dit
Der hat mie geliebt, der über
Liebe spotten Kann - Tras
J.C La viater .... das gedicht
an die Pflaumenblüte erhob
einen verbannten münster
Hong Kong cueille comme un japonischen gott
Wenn der Wind aus nordost
weht bringt er den Duft der
Pflaumenblüte mit -
Ist euer Herr auch nicht
daheim vergess nicht dass
oder frühling Schloss naht .... le
Luxembourg létrône —
phare de Lichtenstein le joyeuse
de l'Europe son pont na bitel,
dessiner le nid de flamingo
rose et ses œuf blancs, rose bleus
rouges sur la cheminée du château
de la famille Mozart à l'orgue

le pays des amours où fleurit
l'oranger sur une robe de sa
tin blanc et un diadème de
fleur de diamants de roses
en nacre Que i-t Marc Churchill
millefleur Chamore C marguerite
Eglise de Saint Jean Eglise Vaduz
Ave Maria le fruit de tous
sein rose et béni soit béni
entre nous tous. l'adorons
a personne de l'église en perle
d'l'écrin le cathédrale est
declarée reine de la lumière
baise main et du manteau
de pourpre Le soleil va baiser
toutes les fleurs avec ton nom
de Marguerite en bouquet
de diamant à Marie Louise
— Cuit de Noël de madame
selle Nathalie au saint vient
— La nuit comme un fruit éclate
Ses fruits sont le rire heureux des pul
pes d'or des raisins bleus où chant
et i vine une agathe. — Les fruits
de la nuit féconde lucarnes du
miracle en fleurissant laisté
on cette la terre fleurie de l'espace. —

...sur notre monde l'invisible
ourlé de splendeur – de Noël. Ils
se sonnne, harmonies. Bruisse-
ment d'ailes bénies – Ruisselle-
ment d'astres, d'anges ... – Petit
enfant... – Roi rayonnant un
Lys endormi sur l'humble
chaume. les cœurs et l'a-
mour sont promus –

Denise Dupras –

École de nonne de Saint Louis
son "Noël" p. les petits – C'est dans
la nuit de noël qu'une étoile
guide les mages vers un très
petit village, vers un très
pauvre hôtel. C'est à la fête de
Noël que les enfants de tous
les âges promettent d'être bien
bien sages avec un air très
solennel. Pourquoi j'aime
noël – c'est notre fête la
fête des petits enfants. Ils ont
des plaisirs pleins la fête et plein
le cœur aussi. Vraiment j'aime
Noël. Vous le Bon Enfant
en trône d'élephant... cadeau j'aime la
fête familière où l'on oublie nos

la ville Éternelle reflet l'Italie
heureuse Byron l'appelait
Cité de l'âme, le paradis sur
terre ouvrage Paléologue
Rome cette ville magique
ses palais de pierre en
dentelles et ses merveilleux
tableaux d'opérations 1 pages
Saint Pierre vu du château
Saint-Ange qui tient une épée
dans le fourreau ... l'Arc de
Constantin ou ellipse de sou-
verains sur des collonnades
roses — en républiques des
papes dont on manteau.
l'annonciation à Noël chante
ave Maria gratia plena
bénit soit le fruit de ton sein rose
La voie Sacrée du Vatican a
perdu ses chariots de fruits et
ses défilés triomphaux
du haut du Mont Mario
ils applaudissaient ... Ô Roma
nobilis, orbis et Domina
Cicérone --- la Bonne
Mère la lampe éternelle des
lumières est aussi Marseille tout

près de Nice. est en folie c'est un
jour de Carnaval les femmes plus
aux bras ... galants se pressent
vers le bal. Et parmi les ...
passent un joli domino un
Pierrot fantasque lui murmure quelques mots, c'est si doux
d'écouter ce qu'il dit qu'aussi-
tôt la femme le suit sur un
lit de fleurs le Titien il osa retirer
son masque de velours. Au bord
de la Riviera on murmure une
brise embaumée chaque
femme a rêvé là-bas d'être belle
et toujours adorée dans le ciel
jusqu'au firmament les violons
jettent leurs mélodies Sont si doux
les serments ... finals les amants
C'est l'amour qui s'avance en
chantant tout bas là bas au
bord de la Riviera . . . . . . De
son front virginal vient de tour
ber une couronne de bouton de
fleur d'oranger. Elle prie elle
pardonne et puis s'endort
dans un baiser en Impératrice
des roses. — étendue sous les roses.

TO MADEMOISELLE ROSINE
after 1942

To Mademoiselle Rosine
You are tall and just like the
corn in May. And your hand is
not any wider than a rose. As for your
feet my dear child it is another thing
The prince who married Cinderella would have loved
it_   As an   artist   the
gesture is good, the tone formed And you
    sing   how would I say ?   as a
virtuoso.   And you have already well before being hatched. A little taste of you
piquant and perfumed.   I know that
you are ten years old Mademoiselle
And that you are big and that one must
sculpt one's verses : If you were to not find them
good would you enjoy them?   You are
my baby quite nearly my wife
accept my homage and receive
Madame, without blushing of the present,
               as a student
this cornucopia of bonbons
    by Albert Mérat......
    It is   a   love song of Napoleon's
the sun shines on all the almond trees of
Naples where the lovers always take their
marriage oaths - the friends of the espoused
voyaging from the Orient: among the cliffs

orange tree flowers do not leave my

arms in the ballets of the party of Ortigosa

French folk, you are some brave ones

when   France opens its arms

the lighthouses ablaze   illuminating   of   the Isle of the Cross

or   the Isle of Pen Mesa, protect like

let us pluck up the Siren

a bright star on the brow of

F r a n c e   All to the lighthouse

or red let us fish-out the Siren

of the Malibran

Liberty who will bloom again when

she   opens her arms   her   cor-

set of gold and her royal manteau

bring Victoria Hall to its knees within

its military auditorium. Some other

song stanzas of the new year

of the Bon - Enfant and his gifts

time   passes   love   remains

of the miraculous fish

the scepter and the brodequin of Thalie

All flourishes under the flowering scepter

of Bonaparte and his torn flowered manteau of

of the rejuvenation of the balasters

sanpietrina of Saint Pierre

of flowers of fruits of nature of

blue granadilla of   Sans-Souci

or of the imperial crown of the

Sallz of the rose orchids of the marriage

de Gaule painter in Paris, or

those of Pregny (Schenk is king) of

the Rosia....   Prayers for Brè
tagne . The wife of the Bard.
The prayer of the kneeling sailors.
Predications which made flower
the July colonnade was illuminated in the Bengal fireworks finale
of parties Venetian clubs flowering
gondolas in lanterns golden Venice
by <u>Jean-Pierre Caillo'ch</u> = was the <u>president</u>
<u>Lebrun</u> and his theatrical loggia. . .
the queen is brunette
French Chaplain soldier and Breton poet-
his wife Lecorre in Montbenon
in Lausanne, gigantic veil
of crimson from flowered parade floats of the students, In consecrating the flags
she had the air of being taken
in triumph France when Lord God
the orchestra conductor after his Òpera
solo ? presented her a
brought up
bouquet of lilies as he kneeled . her long
train of the queen in her
Carriage (some American bagpipes
in Paris following the example of the beauty
queens of the ballets of the 12 Camellia
women) or also dressed her
heraldic
in the apotheosis of a manteau of
crimson which glorifies the Francophone

Switzerland./. At the Pope's in A-
vignon - Orange and Nice
the royal earth opens up in a flower
thrown into the space   in
battalions of flowers and sings
the sun the sky bed and
the sea Madonna in
in the great blue in the ribbons
a thunderous trio _ the mon-
under her dais she goes to sleep happy
ument of Montreux chief
millefleur
Yersin who as a chanteuse put
some if in a bottlesh-
aped with Englishmen in all her
audiences - - - - I recommend you to God dear angel   She
did not remain like a
Cypress upon the tomb of humanity without the theatrical parties
in marriage of the épées above   her
gift of a jewelry box, a diadem of pearls
of diamonds. One senses the lion
in the darkness who constructed an Achilleion de Corfou of her.
Christomanos spoke Greek to her
arm in arm
to kiss her as money-changer
          Tollebouquine: God be with
you dream angel in the Achilles
I recommend you to God my dear angel Elisabeth

(left vertical margin, bottom to top) under the Panzi Rung the royal ostensory earth

                    or in   an
    heel   or   a   living   ship
        one senses the lion emerges from the darkness
      dal sol Minerva Sédia.
                      swooning
    would fall on him in the belt of Eros
    of the Gürtelrose of the Rubens atelier

      Hollandais painter . I am lov-
    ingly and passionately at your si-
    de in his lively <u>pastoral symphony</u>

    in Armide rose at the chateau
    of Montaulieu (of Beaulieu). Rosa
    lie of the Chablière   in painting
    on your table of the sun in the garden
    of Beau-Soleil in the pension of the
    prof Bernardin de Saint Pierre. One
              Servidumbre del César
     <u>kissed</u> the <u>monastic</u> manteau of
    <u>la Folda</u> de Pie XII of Romeo and
                Chateau d'Ouchy
    Juliette . in flowered gondola or
    kneeling the king of Naples at the

    feet of Zita in the balconies of the almond
    trees, magnolia trees or cherry apricot
    trees peach trees made her necklaces and ear-
    rings which cost no more than a
    kiss. and the song: her two arms
    served her as ladders for climbing
    (on the organs) up on the cherry tree
    from where I smiled at the beauty who

    extended her apron to me and her
    crimson and vermillion fruits I was

(left margin, vertical:) nature of the manteau immense h

ripple of love when the roses are bloomed

making her to amuse her some necklaces, some
earrings that cost   nothing
but a kiss Of the spring in bloom
the first breezes blowing in the
plains and on the slopes It is necessary for
the amorous and the birds to see the
cherries ripen...   .... I was
two years older than Rose
little spirit she had it all I knew
well one thing was to love her
very much to see her to love her to tell
her was the refrain of my heart
in   her   regard   in   her   smile
I saw my happiness come alive
_ _ To celebrate you dear momma
I have put my flowered dress
on the manteau at the Isle of Pans
was painted spring.   On
my face the most pretty smile.
I have donned my most elegant ribbon
in   presenting   my   homage
a blue granadilla in my hand
all sorts of bouquets . . . .
my darling a batterfley bouquetts
a rose over your corall lips-
for their Husbandring diamond
that open in flower showing its manteaux
floral wreath of the royal earth im

78

mense ostensory
in a kiss on the hand from the Walewska at

Finkenstein and the arms in necklaces
from her on Napoleon reposed on the
canapè . . . . . he tears up the rose
garlands   Oberwaid   tears up
the sails   sentimental out-
pouring in   8   idyllic tabl-
eaux The Sun speaks to the earth and says to it
Never has loved the one who can
                                          wake up in

Flout about Love   my arms
JC Lavater . . . . said this
the poem to the bloom of plums
ennobles a banished Minister
                        Thron + Ile
of Hong-Kong picked like a blueberry fruit
to be the Japanese God . -
When the wind blows from the
north east it brings the scent of
Plum blooms with it . . .
Also if your sir is not at
home   do not forget   that
the   Spring nears the....the
                        castle
Luxembourg the throne---
beacon of Lichtenstein the jewel
of Europe its natural bridge,
to draw the pink flamingo
nest and its eggs white, rose blue
red on the chimney of the chateau
of the family Mozart at the organ

(left margin, vertical) in heraldic flower   song   out   rose--   last   which spreads

the country of the loves where flowers
the orange tree on a white satin
dress and diadem of diamond
flowers of mother of pearl
roses ,   Queen and Marg Churchill
millefleur Chamorel = Marguerite
Church of Saint Jean Church of Vaduz...
Ave Maria   the fruit of your
rose and blessed bosom ; blessed be
among us all.   We adore
you in church in pearls
in the   cathedral   coffer   is
declared queen of the light
kiss on the hand and of the manteau
of crimson   The sun will kiss
all the flowers with your name
of   Marguerite in   bouquets
of diamonds to Marie Louise
Night of   Noël   Mademoi
selle   Nathalie   or saint night
The night like a fruit explodes
ripe
Its ruptures are the happy laughter of the gol
den pulps of blue grapes where sings
and irizates an agathe. ... The ruptures
of the fecund night skylight of the
miracle flowering have left
one throws the flowery earth in the space-

choir upon our world the invisible
embroidered- Noël splendor. God
gives himself harmonies. Rust-
ling of blessed wings. Streaming of celestial excited bodies...Little
                    of angels in
child . King without kingdom a
      lamp - - of fire
Lily asleep on the humble
thatch . the hearts and the l-
ove   are promoted
            Denise Dupraz -
School of the nun of Saint Louis
It's Noël for children--It's in
the night of Noël that a star
guides the magi towards a very
small village and towards a very
                Lotus   like
poor hotel. It is during the fête of
     the daughters of Emmaüs
Noël that the children   of all
ages promise to be
well behaved with a very
solemn air. Why do I love
Noël . It is our fête the
fête of little children. They have
simple pleasures filling their mind and filling
their heart as well   really I love
          to see the Bon-Enfant
Noël for its mystery its secrets and
     on the elephant throne
its beautiful presents I love the
familial party where we forget our

shortcomings

81

the Eternal city reflection of happy
has its brodequin
Italy   Byron   called°of it the
City of soul, the paradise on
is its work
earth: Maurice Paléologue
flowered
Rome this magical city
its palaces of intricate
stone patterning and its marvellous
and of the marvels of the ancient world
tableaux of the adoration of the Magi
has the air of a flower plucked on the stone
Saint Pierre seen from the chateau
Saint Ange which replaced an épée
in the sheath . . . The Arch of
Constantine or ellipse of sov-
ereigns on the rose collona-
des- in republic of the
its three rose marble steps __
popes. in his manteau . .
the annunciation for Noel sings
Ave Maria Gratia pleina
blessed be the fruit of your rose bosom
The Sacred path of the Vatican has
of Tespis
lost its chariots of fruits and
its victory marches.
from the height of Monte Mario
she speads
they were applauding...Ô the Roma
nobilis, orbis et Domina by
Cicerone ____ the Bonne
queen
Mère the eternal lamp of the
lights is also Marseille very
from

close to **Nice**. is rapturous it's a
day of Carnival the beautiful women
in the arms of gentlemen hasten
towards the ball. and among the masks
pass un joli domino noir
whimsical pierrot muttering
a couple of words to her, it is so sweet
to listen to him that the woman
promptly follows   him   to   a
bed of flowers the Titien he dared remove
his   velvet   mask   .   Along
the **Riviera** one murmurs
a   balmy   breeze   each
woman has dreamed there of being beautiful
and always adored in the blue
up to the heavens the violins
throw their laments Are so sweet
the sermons always faithful the lovers
This is love that marches on
singing softly down there
along side the Riviera.... From
her virginal brow comes to fall
a   crown   of   flower   buds   of
orange tree flower. She prays
she pardons and then goes to sleep
in   a   kiss   as   the   Empress of
of roses - stretched out beneath the roses

Meyerling

83

FÊTE DES VIGNERONS
1944

Ô Cérès : Mais qui nous a donné
l'abondance où nous sommes
Voyez ce char traîné par des boeufs
lents et ... Salut déesse des
blémis Ô mère ô nourrice des
hommes. À la voir la foule
accourue envahit inonde les champs
à toi la herse et la charrue creu-
sant des sillons fécondés - bis
Cérès à toi [les trônes de la terre]
la ruche des abeilles qui d
tes fleurs vont butiner
leur miel Cérès à toi les fruits
de nos corbeilles à toi les voeux
qui s'élèvent au ciel Cérès alors
les fruits de tes corbeilles à toi les
voeux qui s'élèvent au ciel - la

Cérès à toi les peuples de la
terre qui dans tes bras en
(char de la Malibran) berça
l'humanité qui dans tes
bras berça l'humanité -
Les chemins sont parés de berceaux d'é
glantines qui de la source au loin abri-
te les secrets Et la fleur qui s'entr'ouvre au som
met des collines de suaves senteurs embaume

+ Cérès à toi les paroles de la terre
~tu~ ~seras~ ~toujours~ ~la~ ~patronne~
en reine de charité Et les bluets
de ta couronne fleuriront toujours dans les blés Tu seras
toujours la nourrice et la
mère qui dans tes bras berça l'humanité, qui dans tes
bras berça l'humanité.
Ô Bacchus refrain 2° strophe : Il re-
chauffe la reine du pauvre laboureur il couronne la
tête royale du poète
rêveur (coureur de la fête des Bacchus peints de Pâques) = Par son
charme il enchaîne de roses
l'heureuse humanité = bis
l'heureuse humanité ——
Une rose au front de Victorie en chantant
Elle naquit en Mai quand la rose est éclose
pris le nom tant aimé si doux de rose
Et sa taille de Vénus gracieuse élancée
tenait entre deux doigts et pouvait être
pressée . = Aussi les amoureux é
taient nombreux = 3 ou 4 fois — —
Ne partez pas déjà ne quittez pas mes
bras l'heure est si belle, profitons d'elle
ne partez pas — J'ai disposé pour vous plaire

qui importe à qui une autre heure apporte — —

les fleurs que vous préférez. Une trainée de
lumière laisse des éclats mordorés
pour exhausser ma prière vers moi re-
nez reposer — J'guette avec impatience
ce votre arrivée de chaque jour et vos
instants de présence me semblent toujours
trop courts. Chérie ne dites pas adieu restez encore un peu — fermer la porte
et restez là ce soir seul compter la joie qui
monte nous grisera —

Créador Requiem fils de la nuit

destins d'or qui au te vorera en
God is our refuge am strange Trost
fois Dieu est notre haute retraite —
Lohengrin — fliegen mit Engel im paradis — Der Kna-
be schläft am grünen gesta-
de. Ich führe ihn auf Orquel
im schatte — spielen
die wasser um die Lust
wir lachten mit voller
Lust bunds colossal-
rosen Kranz érum ver-
tingt der Knabe in der
grünt... Ich locke der
Knabe ich — griffe herein
deux fois und fliegen
mit Engel im Paradies.
Und es ruft aus der tie-
fen Cléopatha de "rubis lieb+

Ô Bacchus

Moi dont les mains toujours
prodiguées (s'enrichissent) pourvoir de bienfaits
renaissants d'un généreux salaire
2 Souris Bacchus à ces accents —
1 En payant nos fatigues. Souris
Bacchus à ses accents — bis
Dans la cité d? le simple village
lisons chaque toit tu nous
portes nectar retremper
la force du jeune âge et ne
trouves la force du vieillard
tu donnes à le jeunesse et
joie et santé tu donnes à la
vieillesse des éclairs des é-
clairs de gaîté tu donnes
à la souffrance un rayons
séducteur un rayons sé-
ducteur ô Bacchus ô Bac
alors tu fleurit la colline
et l'enivrante extase et les ardeurs divines
transporte l'homme aux cieux, bis —
l'Impératrice danse d? le manteau de bal
l'Empereur avec Napoléon 1er
dans le lit des fleur de Véron
tu cherche l'homme en fleur
quadrille 4 mains Sacha Guitry

ou Élève de Brienne — 4 mars
orchestre sous la direction de
Esn parent cathédrale
Meyrous trouvera en radio
les paroles — — valses-
ström en ouverture —
la Sainte Lrunsi est
préférable également
avec paroles. — Zaïre
Rendez la robe a César le Titien
+ il réchauffe la veine du
pauvre laboureur il cou-
ronne la tête du poète rêveur
(après les coureurs) — Sur ses pas
il entraîne la pauvre hu-
manité par son charme
enchanteur. — deux fois —
2e strophe de Ô Bacchus +

Enguirlande Napoléon d° l'É-
néïde en Bon Enfant d° les
voile de fleur cérébrale de mon pays de sa
fiancée écrins des fiançailles
la fée magique du Kiosque
lui lance des fleurs au visage,
sur l'échelle de fleurs de lys au
Château d'amour d'Estavayer

89

Gounod   Marie Stuart   Le va-
ave maria

... Je t'adore ô Soleil quand tu jette des roses
dans l'air... Après ces semaines bénies qui ont fuis comme
le vent... Il me faut repren-
dre la chaîne entre quatre murs
m'enfermer.... entre quatre
murs m'enfermer — je
jette des roses et des palmes
sur les processions front cent
de voiles toutes couronnées de
roses à ... Noël de guerre —

austerlitz... ce serait bon de
renaître ... au bonheur dont
s'imprégnait jadis la nuit
du Saint Mystère Et d'en-
tendre chanter Noël en votre
honneur jusqu'au bout
de la terre — je me souviens
des beaux Noël des temps ja-
-dis — Quand sous nos yeux pas-
saient les plus belles images
des Noël évoquant tout un
bleu paradis l'étoile et
les rois mages — je me
souviens des beaux Noël

90

où des bergers cheminaient
dans mon rêve au devant
de la crèche Où l'Enfant
s'endormait sous des souffles
légers parmi la paille fraîche
— D'autres accents que ceux
de l'orgue ou du beffroi im-
périeusement frapperont
nos oreilles Rumeurs aux
longs échos de douleurs et
d'effroi à des tocsins pareilles
— par andré pierre Humberto
Oh! ne voulez vous pas accorder aux humains de revivre
un Noël d'ombre et d'alarmes
Un Noël où la Paix Wilson et son
union féminine comme
un bouquet de fleurs d'o-
ranges! de ses divines mains
étancherait les larmes —
De toute part alors au penchant
des côteaux des clochers égre-
naient des chansons solennelles Et
des lumières d'or des orgues
sitôt l'extase en nos prunelles
Des chants joyeux vibraient à l'en-
tour des maisons Un parfum

de résine errait au long des rues Car l'étoile
était là vibrante à l'horizon dès la
nuit apparue – Aujourd'hui les clochers vont tressaillir encore Des
tons psaumes diront de graves harmonies – mais l'ombre fermira le pur
et beau décor de la mer ce infinie –
Des cris se mêleront aux cantiques
fervents Des sanglots trahiront
la détresse des misères Et plus haut
que nos voeux rouleront dans
le vent des paroles amères Oh !!
ne voulez vous pas Seigneur en cette
nuit dont la flamme vacille
au milieu des Ténèbres (Post Tenebras
lux) Délivrez notre coeur et nos
yeux pleins d'ennui – de leurs
ombres funèbre – – Oh !! ne
voulez vous pas accorder aux
humanités un Sapins de Noël
au studio de Richemont ou au
amphithéâtres des fêtes vénitiennes au Palace Anibry –
mascarade sur la mer –
Voici Noël ô douce nuit l'é-
toile est la qui nous conduit (dans
le manteau de bal) allons donc tous
avec les mages porter à Jésus vos hom
mages un Sauveur ne est né car
l'Enfant nous est né – L'an
nore et la nuit du tombeau de Médicis
le jour et le crepuscule a Bonne Michel Ange
<u>La Traviata</u> enlevée à le train bleu –

Marguerite de Bourgogne
et la danse au conciela, Manon a Saint Sulpice l'organiste à genoux une porteuse de
pain enlevée dans le ca-
rrosse d'Amiens (qui est mieux
dans une yole à rideau, trion
s'endormir en Corinne à côté
le roi minette de Portici, Manon
Les Caux (délaisse l'Hôtel de Caux
je t'ai raris — a Pavia en
Sonnambula = Zaira d
le sarail — mon beau vaisseau d'amour (navette) Marinella]
viens d° mes bras chanter jusqu'an jour danser d° ta robe d'a-
mour (la rumba d'amour —
Rosita Manon bouquet
de fleurs de lumière d'artifices d° la main — des orgues
Anita brunette — Bouquetière
effleurait son nom en
Margherita Santa —
Hôtel joli gentil frou frou
d'Hella danseuse chanteur de
Pierre Chamlaine (un la Cordeaux
ses deux bras lui servait d'échelle

pour monter pour le cerisier des
colliers de ses bras de Bonne
porte et de ses fruits sur leur
casaques qui ne lui coû-
taient qu'un baiser — Je
t'aime Ô la nuit bras en croix tant
beaucoup à le poli ko fragonard
grisette du couvent l'Apsara
de tout mon pays étais n'êtes reine je suis roi
de *Folie-Bergère* suppose de
donne ma vie — Je
la porte sur traîne d'éléphant
et de je tiens corso fleuri
écoutant chantes en Nadio
le roi t'amuse à la montres
de tous les théâtres — de Carnaval de Venise mas-
carade sur la mer en
Sédia de la grande bleue
Notre dame de la Rosée de
l'Hôtel de la rosière en Corse —
jolie et Venise la belle
et Venise d'or — et la gentille
fille de Grenade ton Fernand
qui t'attend ici l'air d'Opéra
il vient il vient Ferdinand
roi soleil illuminait l'Europa

fait refleurir la porte de la
terre la parer en fleurs d'archange
de Gambetta l'enveloppa
d'un manteau Impérial
d'ses bras — Dans un baiser
la jeune femme a senti son
front virginal brûlant d'une
enivrante flamme et puis
dans ce lit nuptial vient de
tomber une couronne
de boutons de fleur d'oranger,
elle prie le préttan trône Miche-
lier elle pardonne et puis s'en
dort, la rose la plus belle se doit
du qu'on rit tout — dehors
du couvent en mariage d'Ismet Pacha — ou Czartorisky au
Château d'Ouchy Palace Beau-Ri-
vage..... Dans un bouton de rose
mon cœur est enfermé per-
sonne en a la clef que toi seul
mon bien aimé seulement
a Demantour de Nesle — d²
le pensionnat marie Stuart de la Kenthaler
Le bouquet de l'équière Ville
prend sa tête diamant d'artiste Pluie
les deux épouse au pieds de la croix
de Kervadec rendaient du balcon

de Geneviève de Candia
Le colibri et le grand Pardon
de Ploërmel opéra les mariés
se donnaient la main à l'église
ils portait le rayon de rose en
ils avaient l'intention de Byron
d'avoir rencontré leur voiles —
mes dans le tracé de fleur d'o-
ranger avec leur robe blanche telle
une grande fleur de la Piégessalle
de Paris Souci en collier de la
perle-rose de l'Inde - a toutes
les statue de Marbre au lit des
roses ou un monument insigne
de Marbre en la portant plusieurs étudiants
sur son beau vaisseau d'amour
(du cygne noir ou blanc) du beau
Danube bleu horizons bleus de ses
grands yeux bleus Isten velled
azcrett angylom — vaincu de
vant ce marbre ô Vesta j'ai
soulevé tes voiles nuptiale parure
de l'angleterre fleurie Elisabeth
Quand le colibri chante on enlève à tra-
vers les fenêtres sa mariée exprès
pour vous celle papillon a la fleur de
lys exprès pour vous s'ouvrent les
roses sur le balcon dans le matin

l'ell tombé sur moi je l'écoute
chanter atala dans le imonte au
impérial à la Carla — Les Walkhyria
de Wagner. Il va montrer sa tête —
royale à genoux au pieds de la diablesse mère d° le manteau de pourpre
me supplie de m'épouser [ou]
Siegfried au clair de lune au milieu des fleurs d'amarylis] couché
sur sa graciella d° la grotto di Po
-lo tel l'ascenstrasse grotte au fée
magique grand papillons quand
Hella relève ses toutes ailes en l'air au milieu
couleurs il étale Fernand son
manteau de brocard sur le lit de la
Chypris. avec un ange d° le ciel de
lit de Marie Antoinette. Où la reine
d'Angleterre accoudée au lit à triple
couronnes de Napoléon étendu
en Marceau — à demi mort amour
reine d'elle — Au contraire il est au
pied de la blanche cavale, en sculpteur
de la reine Zita empanachée de plumes
roses et des calas d° le manteau degraffé
de rubis. et le voile et le diadème
d'or de diamant. collyre d° un écrins des
fiançailles qui compose le char des

mariés se lancent ou au monde
le bouquet (final) au monde
en souvenir d'une fleur cueillie
dans la foule en fleur en offrant
multi tourtes de Saint-Rosaire
Le jeu de cartes a prédit le lit nuptial
de Marguerite de Bourgogne -
a moi la seconde manche
des trônes où je toujours de la pension
de Pierrefontaine — ô Marguerite
épousez-moi en doge de Venise je vous
porterai sur les mains d° mon
manteau de cour royal cueillis
la rose de Naples sur deux
Saint Siege pontifical au Lido
méditerranéen — Tout est lumiè-
re dans leur tableau-réclame = Licht de Brodway. Noël des Rois Mages —
Francis Carco = Je te donne
ce coin fleuri ces arbres en
fleur léger cette brume Helli
-Paris qui s'allume sous ces
nuages blancs et gros-
Procession pascale en Es-
pagne Sedia d'anges con-
...ie portée par des papes des fidèles
Préraphaélite ; de monuments...

Se donnaient en tournant un
œuf colorié en colliers ils les
adornait de devises armou
-riées —   Noël des rois Mages
Ce matin j'ai rencontré le train
De trois grands rois qui étaient ~d'amour~
en voyage — Ce matin j'ai rencontré le train de trois grands
rois dessus le grand chemin
J'ai vu d'abord des gardes de corps
Des gens armés avec une troupe
de pages j'ai vu d'abord des gardes
du corps tout dorés sur leurs ~pis~
~tan~corps les drapeaux qui
étaient pour sûrs fort beaux aux
brises servaient d'amusements
Les chameaux qui étaient ~j~
~sûr fort beaux~ portaient des
bijoux tout ~immenses~
les tambours j? faire honneur ~les~
de temps en temps faisaient
bruire leur tapage battaient
la marche chacun son tour
Dans un char doré de toute
part (du Bois Enfant) On
voyait les rois modestes comme
~une~ des anges — On voyait

oreilles de riches étendarts on
entendait des haut-bois de
telles voix, qui de mon
Dieu publiaient les louanges
qui disaient des airs d'un
admirable ... Ébahi d'un
tendre cela je me suis rari
ce jour vois l'équipage de
loin en loin je les ai toujours
suivis l'astre brillant qui
était depuis ... arrêta net
quand il fut a l'enfant
Ils entrent ensuite p? adorer
leur roi à deux genoux
il commencent leurs prières
et reconnaître sa di-
vine loi — Gaspard d'abord
présente l'or il dit mon
Dieu vous êtes le seul roi de gloire
et dit partout qu'il vient
chasser la mort Pour présent
Melchior offre l'encens en
lui disant vous êtes le dieu
terre royale défenseur ...
des ... disant vous êtes
roi fleuri? êtes Dieu tous en-
semble la pauvreté l'hu-
milité ... empêche pas votre

Divinité Chu…nd à moi
j'en pleure la pauvreté et l'hu-
milité de votre amour sont
des preuves certaine Chu…nd
a moi j'en pleure mon bon
Dieu en sanglotant je me
présente la m… …hetes
(mariages) Chu…nd a moi
d'y songer je suis plus mort
que vif un jour pour
moins sur une croix des
organistes ~~sans radio du royal~~
~~Bisogrigi~~— Comme mortel
~~vous puissiez nos misère~~
Vous devrez mourir pour le
salut de tous — en écoutant
leur concerts d'orgues —

Mes enfants voici la fête de Noël
C'est le nouvel an a jour
chacun s'apprête voyez quel
élan l'hiver a sur la nature a
jeté son ~~…~~ manteau . Plus
de fleurs plus de ~~verdure~~ Et
pourtant c'est beau — ~~Hermine~~
Mi nuit chrétien — c'est
l'heure solennelle — com-
me autrefois une étoile brillante

y conduisait les mages d'orient
Mistral et Mireille cos-
tume Toreros espagnols
: Nous sommes en avril les
prés verdissent Les amandi-
ers se couvrent de fleurs
blanches et roses — les
alpilles comme un socle de
granit doré dans le ciel bleu =
les banquises humaine face de
Napoléon dressé sur le monde. les
peuples béants ne purent que se
taire Les bras levés il présentait
à la terre (grand l'aurai je toute
fleurie) son enfant nouveau-né
On dirait le Völkerschlacht —
ou le socle de la Tégess allée il
un phare mystérieux calme plane
dans les cieux on mᵐᵉ de Staël
dansait autour comme une
Liberté tombée de le Völkerschlacht — panier rempli de roses d'a-
mandier le casque le lanterne
de pourpre et d'or au soleil cou-
chants la grande Campeador.
générale désarmement (reste une
revue de banquets et bouquets final

prise en Jane d'arc (moderne
La Catherine rouge à cheval
les cordons de la bannière de
Brocard - inclusivement
à longs pli traînant en couronne-
nant des bannières - Comme
une ceinture de pourpre rive d'Hé-
rode lacée d° des rubans des) merveilles du mondes anciens natu-
relles roulant dedans à ses pieds
l'organiste et fors livre d'Opéras
où ces) Merveilles en roman dà
moun + figure les œuvres de Gounod compositeur: Mireille. Sapho
Faust. Roméo et Juliette Philemon et
Baucis (l' Illumination de la création par
la ville des Lumières de Brodway -
Revieus Jérusalem toute illumi-
née comme Picadilly - la ville des
roses - Copenhague. Amchy bouquet
d'artifices de Bengale. le roman
de la rose Hymne à Marie on
Ave - Maria il golfe di campe de
Venisti. le pape d° sous manteau La
reine de Carthage - la reine de
Saba la reine Esther - Jézabel
La fille de Pharaon - La reine Victoria
la rose en diadème - l'Imperatrice Eli-

sabeth l'Impératrice Eugénie – et
son collier de Château de Reine Ber
the Opéra Sphinxe Victoria
– Cléopâtre – Iphigénie
en Aulide – une sirène
au bord du Nil bleu – un
vrai balustre en collier – du
Capitole – Le Compositeur Gou –
nod – Roméo et Juliette –
Faust son collier de perles rose
de l'Inde Sapho son bouquet
sur le lit de fleur d'oranger –
Werther mariage à l'auto bou –
quet d'orchidée de Prégny Rosita –
Baynlummister Wilhelm II
Iphigénie en aulide
plusieurs ballets et cantatri
ce y jette des fleurs Lindt – Walkyria
are maria – 6 ans –
mme Lohengrin Zila
reste aux pieds avec son
navire en corbeille de mariage
toilette dans son long manteau
en l'enlevant d'une grotte lu –
xieusement meublée –
Debarquement de Cythère
flambeau d'ange Gambetta

blonde d° les bras du général
(état major à genoux — Elle
avait l'air aussi d'un ange de
marbre blanc des processions
pascales en Espagne —
les en angle blanc très haute
comme les voile d'un bateau de
peintre bouches — l'air encore
d'un flambeau des mer-
— veilles du monde dans
ses voiles nuptials — dans
son manteau Impérial
madame de Staël (l'univers
c'est à elle Weltall dir geschenk
Napoléon ihr geben K —
Delphine Corinne de l'Allemagne — l'ange se trouve
dans le nom Charlema-
gne et ses madone 7 couronnes
de 7 merveilles du monde ancien
iliatiques — une grande Eu-
ropéenne — et son gigan-
tesque velum de pourpre sur
Versaille-Français russe — et vau-
dois à Canse sur le palais du Krem-
lin Alexandra — sur le Palais de Bu-
à l'air d'une langue qui se dresse en égypte
même est recouvert du couronne-
ment des bannières et du dra-

...peau géant à ½ banderolles rouges et 48 étoiles sur l'extrême pointe
des Capitole éclate (ou éclatant) au
vent de l'atlantide — ses por-
tiques d'éléphants ou le maharad
rajah descend du haut de son trône
de Deli plusieurs pachidermes se
couchent pour le roua et
se dressent en airain lançant
à l'espace les chars de la victoire et
sa lampe d'or suspendue dans
les bannières d'azur — chinoises
(le sphinx de la Triangelée-ey)
peint dedans en enguirlandant
Bonaparte et ses chars héraldi-
ques fleurs helvétiques s'épanoui-
t sur le manteau de l'Impératrice Elisabeth [sur le Larousse]
sur l'autel de la patrie Suisse a
Montre(ux) d'or des vignes plan-
tée en fleur d'archanges de Saint
Légier marche comme un cygne
et coupe d'argent comme ange nié-
nuphar de ses ailes en l'air cette incon-
arable fleur [d'ansoka] de marbre l'hiver s'an-
crent aux navire de la Bible de la
nature composent les écrins des

chars du Bon Enfant les écrins
des fiancailles du Mahadrajah
collier de perles roses de l'Inde Bazar
Béchart le char des fiancailles
des corso fleuris des fiancailles
l'écrins de phsycho, des palan-
quins de la Béatrice d'Este espagnole
portés le jour de Pâques de l'Opé
ro (bijoux) de terre lita maria Médicis
les musées de peinture gothiques de
la nature. Elle a sa Sédia ou on
lit portatif. La diablesse au balcon,
de l'amphithéâtre des temples de
Jupiter — ou sur la mer — Triton
d'son manteau roule son
— livre d'or de la Création — sous
les baisers du Soleil — en Seigneur resplendissant de lumière a étendu le ciel comme un tapis sur ses pieds
adorés. chaque pages s'ouvri-
rait le manteau déchiré a
Bonaparte; fuse alors les bouquets ou jets d'eau de fleur, de lumière feu de Bengale, de Sans Souci
ci toutes les Siègessalées Colonna
autour de la fleur de mappemonde

comme un bouquet de fleur de
lumière Magnifique unité
lumière (de Broadway) et pu-
reté c'est un rayon des fleurs
(des orgues) cri d'appel au cœurs
                    sainteté sainteté -
Sacrifice de la beauté c'est com
me un chant des fleur
        charité charité par m C.
- Chrysanthème - en musique
petite Geisha chrysanthème au
multiple et changeant miroir
que couronne d'un diadème
les Japonais et les Chinois de
pourpre et d'or toujours coiffée
pour le plaisir du Mikado offrant sa nuque ébouriffée hors
d'adorable Kimonos en d'colori
te immolée sur l'autel ou le banc
fleuri de Lygie et son Ursus - Le vent
des mers souffle d'Asie sur tes
plumets dechiquetés et confère
à leur frénésie une éphémère
royauté. Car tu brandis sur l'hi-
vers blême le sceptre en fleurs
de tes dédains Et meurs en
beauté dernier amour du
jardin - par Isabelle Kaiser an-

tant dire toute la terre s'épanou-
it sous le sceptre fleuri du renou-
veau en robe d'amour d?
on revêt la terre en adorant toujours. Dieu est le nom que tout
adore quand la cime se dore, et
la couvre du manteau é-
clatant de verdure et de vie.

Le dénombrement de Bethlehem
et la fuite en Egypte = Un
ange apparut au songe
a Joseph et lui dit Lève toi
prend le petit enfant et sa mère
fuis en Egypte Mathieu
2 - 13 peinture de Fra Angelico

Quo vadis = (Domine)

J'ai vu fleurir tout beau
ciel d'Italie et les sirè-
nes aux voiles de roses sur
le banc de Lygie couron-
nées dans tes bras en robe
d'amour dont on revêt la
terre... en l'adorant toujours
Dieu est le nom que tout
adore quand la lune se dore
dans son manteau... é-
tait de verdure et de vie en
ō colombe im-
molée sur l'autel

mise en scène la Vénus de Milo de
fête de théâtre avait teint en diablesse son manteau de cour royal
du diadème du Sauveur robe
de papillon de paphos - de né-
nuphars — d° le lit des roses -
baiser les statues de marbre
en toilette de Vénus — reste témoi-
rement de Jupiter dans les guirlandes
de roses de la psyché lui a lancé -
Elle lui jette des fleurs au visage -

1 acte   <u>ô Palès</u>   la Fête des Vignerons

Le Zéphir printanier ranime la verdure le divin rossignol sur les
jeunes rameaux redis son hymne à la nature Et l'alerte ber-
ger. fatigué du repos au pâturà
jeaunè reconduis ses troupeaux

Palès déité des prairies étends sur
les rives fleuries de tes nouveaux
présents un odorant trésor. Revêt,
de tes couleurs et les monts et
la plaine dans les champs au bord
Sur l'aspect et dans les champs au bord
flot — le cristal des fontaines tout reflets,
à l'envi bondir des cieux
joùnne à la brise un doux essor
Et l'oiseau d'élan plus agile — — =
au bord du lac tranquille
[Et les anges ont] le sourire des cieux †
La primevère éclate en bouquet
gracieux la primevère éclate
en bouquets en bouquets
gracieux — ô Bacchus — Solo —
ô Bacchus.. ô Bacchus ô Bacchus
ô Cérès vous enguirlandez l'autel
de la nature, [dans tes bras] Enivrez
la suite de Sol; = La violette à Schil-
ler — La terre est son ouvrage | Jupîtes
est son partage | le Créateur | Jupîtes
figure sur sa main

WINEGROWER'S FESTIVAL
1944

<u>Ô Cérès</u>: Month that has given us
the abundance where we are
See this carriage hauled by cattle
slow and steady...Salute goddess of the
ripened wheat ô mother ô nursemaid of
men . To your voice the over
running crowd inundated the fields
to you the harrow and the plow- holl-
owing the fecund furrows- repeat
[Cérès to you [the thrones of the earth]
the hive of the bees who to
your flowers go to gather
their honey Cérès to you the fruits
of our baskets to you the wishes
that rise to the heavens Cérès to you
the fruits of your baskets to you the
wishes that rise to the heavens _

<u>Cérès to you</u> the people of the
earth who in your arms (in
(carriage of the Malibran) cradled
humanity who in your
arms cradles humanity --
ô Palés ___)
The paths are adorned with cradles of
sweetbriar that from the far-off source house
the secrets And the flower which opens up at the sum
mit of the hills of sweet fragrances perfumes

(left margin, vertical) forests the perfumes

(right margin, vertical) of fragrance perfumed of sweet - of the forest

+<u>Céres</u> to you the people of the earth
on the hand of Jupiter
You will always be the patron
queen of charity And the cornflowers
of your crowns will always flourish in the wheatgrasses You will always
be the nursemaid and the
mother who in your arms cradled humanity who in your
arms cradled humanity.
<u>Ô Bacchus</u>   refrain 2nd stanza : he wa-
rms the veins of the poor la
borer he crowns the
royal head of the poet of the poet
dreamer (runner of the fête of the Butcher Easter painter) = By his
charm he strings together roses
happy humanity . repeat
<u>happy humanity</u>
singing
A rose on the brow of Victoria at the ball
She was born in May when the rose is blossomed
took the name most beloved and sweet of the <u>rose</u>
And her waist of Venus gracious willowy   I
held her between two fingers and without
haste . - Also the lovers w-
ere numerous = 3 or 4 times ___
Do not leave already don't leave my
arms the hour is so beautiful let us enjoy it
don't leave - I have arranged to please you

what does it matter to me that one imparts that which another hour provides...

116

the flowers that you prefer A very soft
light leaves bronze slivers
to fulfill my prayer towards me
come rest – I impatiently await
your arrival each day and your
moments of presence seem to me always
too short. Dear don't say adieu stay a little more – close the door .
and stay here tonight all that matters is the joy that
mounts intoxicates us . Don't leave

Toreador Requiem son of the night of the
God is on refuge . Peärea -
destin Don Juan le Toréros sur les lèvres
Athenea refuge and strange
God is on refuge and strange-threetimes
God is our high retreat -
- Lohengrin title. flying with Angels in Paradise - the boy
sleeps at the green verge
I lead him to Orguel
in the shadow _ the waters
congregate around the chest
we laugh with wild
Ecstasy   both colossal
roseWreath olivetree entombed the Boy in the
crypt ... I entice the
Boy _ I _ reel him in _
two times...and flying
with Angel in Paradise
And it calls from the dep
ths Cléopatra of rubies loved

you are mine –

Ô Bacchus

You whose hands always
enrich themselves
profligate for us with good deeds
reborn from a generous salary
2 Smile Bacchus at these accents...
1 In paying for our woes . Smile
Bacchus at his accents . repeat
In the city in the simple villi
age under each roof you come
through your nectar to rejuvenate
the force of young age and recover the force of the elderly
You give youth its
joy and health you give old
age thunder glints
of gaiety you give
suffering a seduc
tive beam a seduc
transport man to the heavens
tive beam ô Bacchus ô Ba
chus you flower the hill from your precious nectar
both intoxicating ecstasy and the divine ardors
transport man to the heavens repeat
The Empress dances in the ball - manteau
with
The Emperor Napoleon
in the bed of the flowers of Néron
on the earth
you seek the blossoming man
quadrille 4 hands Sacha Guitry

and cotillions

ballet

in toilette of Venus at the center of the ballets

as <u>Student of Brienne</u> -4 hands
orchestra under the direction of
Cathedral Emperor
Aleyroux will find in radio
the words to _ waltz
storm as overture...
La Lauterbrunn is
equally preferable
with words.. Zaira
<u>Return the dress to Cesar</u> the Titian
He warms the veins of the
poor laborer he   cro

Ô Bacchus

wns the head of the poet dreamer
(at Easter the runners)-On his steps
he carries along the poor humanity by his enchanting
charm   -   two times -
<u>2nd stanza of Ô Bacchus +</u>
Garland Napoleon in the A
eneid as Bon Enfant in the
floral hoop veils of the
of my country
fiancée engagement coffer
<u>the magic fairy of the Kiosk</u>

throws flowers at his face
on the scale of fleurs de lys of the
Château of love of Estavayer

Gounod Marie Stuart The va-
ave Maria
cations just finished what. Marie
I adore you ô sun when you throw roses
Stuart already to return to the con-
in the air
vent ... after these blessed w
eeks which have fleeted like
the wind.. I must pick up the
chain again between four walls
to enclose me... between four
walls to enclose me____I
throw roses and palms
on the processions brow encircled
of veils all some crowns of
roses on Easter Noël of war procession
Austerlitz
____How sweet it would be to
add
be reborn to happiness which
long ago impregnated the night
of the Mystery Saint And to hear
Noël sung in your
honor until the end
of the earth _ I remember
the beautiful Noëls of times long
ago - When under our eyes passed the most beautiful images
of Noël evoking an entire
blue paradise the star and
the Magi kings_____I re
member beautiful Noëls

where the shepherds walked
In my dream before
the crèche Where the Child
fell asleep under the soft
breaths among the fresh straw
        Other accents that of
the organ or the belfry Im-
        periously will strike
our ears   Rumors
slowly echo of dolor and
of terror at the same tocsins
___by andré pierre humberto
Oh, don't you want to grant
        humans reliving
                exempt
a Noël of darkness and of alarms
A Noël where the Pax\Wilson and his
feminine union like
a bouquet of orange
flowers of his divine hands
would stanch out the tears___
From all sides then
belltowers sounded solemn
songs on the hill sides
                        of organs
And golden lights immediately illuminated
                                eyes
the ecstasy in our ecstasy in our
Joyous songs vibrated all rou
        nd the houses   A perfume

of resin wandered along the streets For the star
was there vibrant at the horizon as soon as the
night appeared   -   Today the bell -
towers will startle again Some
voices will chant the solemn harmonies but darkness will tarnish the pure
and beautiful decor of infinite snow___
Some cries will mix in the fervent
canticles   Lamentations will expose
the distress of the mothers And higher
than our wishes will roll in
the wind the bitter words Oh !!
do you not want Savior in this
night whose flame vacillates
in the middle of the darkness (Post Tenebras
Lux) To deliver our heart and our
eyes full of ennui   -   from their
gloomy darkness _ _ Oh! do
you not want to grant to the
humans a Christmas Tree
at the Studio of Richemont or at the
ampitheaters of Venetian -
fêtes at the Palais d' Ouchy
mascarade on the sea
  Here is Noël ô sweet night the s
tar is there which drives us (in
the ball manteau) let us all go then
with the magi to bring to Jesus our ho
mages a Savior is born to us for
the Child is born to us -- The au-
rora and the night of the tomb of Medicis
the day and the twilight at Rome by Michel-Ange
The Traviata abducted in the blue train

Marguerite de Bourgogne
and the Lady of the Camellias Manon at Saint Sulpice the kneeling
organist a lady bread carrier
captured in the carriage
of Dämiens   (she is mine)
in a skiff made of drapery of the throne
to fall asleep as Corinne next to
of the king mute of Portici Manon
LesCaux (deserts the Hôtel de Caux)
I have kidnapped you in Pavia in
Somnebula = Zaïra in
the seraglio- my beautiful love
vessel operette Marinella
come into my arms to sing until
day to dance in your dress of
love (the rumba of love
Rosita Manon bouquet
of flower of artificial li
ght in the hand - organs
A brunette - Flower girl
touched lightly her name in
Margherita Santa -
Hôtel (your pleasant frou frou
and hailed hellenic Paris dancer narrator of
Pierre Chanlaine (on the chord also
song) your two arms were used by her as a ladder

Clarisse Harlows

to climb on the cherry tree
necklaces from her arms of Bonaparte and of her fruits on their
helmets that cost her
but a kiss - I
to me your arms in second round
love you Marguerite a bit
of the king a rose under the
very much to distraction co
door of the convent
quettery without the Opera
was you are queen if I am king
not at all a day
surprise of
of folly - Bergère I have
given you my life _ I
put her on an elephant throne
of flowered parade float
and I remain kneeling in
listening to her singing on the Radio
the king amuses himself showing it
in all the theaters _ of Carnival of Venice Mas-
querade / on the sea in
Sédia of the Great blue
Notre dame of the Rosée of
the Hotel de la Rosière in pretty
Corsica and Venice the beautiful
and golden Venice _ and the nice
girl of Grenada your Fernand
who awaits her here the Opera tune
he comes : he comes Ferdinand
sun king illuminating Europe

fragonard

makes blossom the door of the
earth to decorate it in flowers of archangel

of Gambetta to envelope it.
in his Imperial manteau
in his arms _ In a boat
the young woman has felt her
virginal brow burning from an

intoxicating flame and then
in this nuptial bed comes to
fell   a   crown

of orange flower buds
she prays to the Sultan throne Méné
lik she pardons and then falls
the most beautiful rose lasts
asleep in a kiss _ outside
but an ins tant
of the convent in marriage of Is
met Pacha - or Tsartorisky at the
Château d'Ouchy Palais Beau-Ri-
vage ..... In a rosebud

my heart is enclosed no-
one has the key only you
my   beloved   only

At Denan tour de Nesles _ in
Marie Stuart   in the
the boarding school AuKenthaler
The bouquet of the squire Ville
preux her diamond head of artist Knie
the two spouses at the foot of the cross
of Kervadec came from the balcony

of Geneviève of Candia

The hummingbird and the grand <u>Pardon</u>
<u>of Ploërmel</u> _{opera} all the brides and grooms
were holding hands at the church
she wore the name of rose whose
they had the intuition of Byron
brow was encircled with veils
of having encountered their beloved

angels in the path of the orange tree

flowers with their white dresses as

a grand flower of the Siegesallee

of Sans Souci in necklace of the
has his   imperial crown
Indian rose pearl has kissed

the marble statues in the bed of

roses or a monument on them
carrying it many students
of <u>Montreaux on the altar</u>- or

<u>on its beautiful vessel of love</u>

(of the black or white swan) of the beautiful

blue Danube blue horizons of his

grand blue eyes Fare thee well

mature dream angel vanquished be

fore this marble <u>ô Vesta</u> I have

lifted your nuptial veils

flowery England Elizabeth

when the hummingbird sings <u>through -</u>
<u>the windows</u> their bride expressly to

hide the butterfly of you at the fleur de

lys expressly for you the roses bloom
of the Walewska Marie Louise
roses on the balcony in the man-

of her
teau fallen upon me I hear it
asleep as an orchestra conductor
singing atala in the imperial
manteau of Carla - The Walkyrias
of Wagner He will show his royal -
head kneeling at the feet of the naked
sorceresse in the manteau of crimson
begs me to marry me [or
Siegfried in the moonlight amid
the amaryllis flowers] laying
on his graziella in the Grotto dipollo
like the Axenstrasse grotto of the magic
fairy grand butterfly when
or the wings in the air
Hella lifts her veils of a thousand
colors he displays to Fernand his
manteau of deerskin on the bed of
Cyprus . with an angel in the heavenly
bed of Marie Antoinette. One has the queen
of England leaning on the triple crown
bed of Napoleon sprawled out
as half a dead Marceau in love
with her _ on the contrary he is at the
has a broken rump
foot of the white mare as a sculptor
of the queen Zita decorated with rare
plumes and of calas in the unclasped manteau
of rubies and the veil and the golden
diadem flaunt diamonds collyre in an engagement
coffer that composes the carriage of the

Operas of Apollo Gounod

brides and grooms threw to each other or to the world
the bouquet (finale) to the world
in remembrance of a flower picked
in the flowering crowd in offering
multi-tortes of Saint - Rosaire
the card game had foretold the nuptial bed
of Marguerite de Bourgogne
to me the second round +
of the thrones where I get you out of the pension
of Pierrefontaine____ô Marguerite
marry me in Doge of Venice I will
carry you on the hands in my
royal court manteau to pick
the rose of Naples on two
Pontific Saint-Seats to the Lido
Mediterranean All is light
in their advertising tableaux= Licht of Broadway - Noël of the Magi Kings -
Francis Carco = I give you
this flowered corner these trees in
light flower this haze Hellenic
Paris which illuminates itself Under these
white and grey clouds -
Easter processions in Sp in white
ain Sedia of angels lay-
ing down carried by popes of the faithful
Preraphaelites of monuments . . .

Were giving themselves in love an
<u>egg colored in collars</u>   he
adorned them with amorous slogans
-his-   Noëls of Magi Kings
This morning I met the train
                              of love
Of three grand kings who were
traveling - This morning I met
the train of the three grand
kings atop the great road
I saw at first body guards
some Armed people with a troupe
of pages I saw first some body
  guards all gilded on their jer-
  kins the flags that were
for sure extremely beautiful in
the breeze served as amusements
The camels that were for
sure extremely beautiful carried some
    and some tortes from the queen Sabaesther
jewels all new And_{repeat}
the drums to pay honor
  from time to time made
rustle their din beating
the march each in his turn
In a <u>gilded carriage</u> of all
part (of the Bon Enfant) One
  saw the modest kings like
        angels - one saw

sparkle of rich standards One

heard from the high-woods some
beautiful voices which of my
^{repeat} (above "voices")

God announced the praises
that (spoke of   airs of an
admirable   of wedding   Astounded to
            party of
hear this I lined up   Noël
        to see the retinue   At
    intervals   I had always
followed them   the shining star
that was ahead stopped dead
          repeat
when he reached The Child
They enter then for to adore
their king^{his}on two   knees
they commence their pra
yers And to recognize his divine rule_ _ Gaspard first
presents the gold and says my
            repeat
God you are the only king of glory
And says everywhere that he comes
to chase death   As a present
Melchior offers   incense in
saying to him you are the god
royal earth immense ostensory
of the armies saying you are
king and you are God all to-
   flowered
gether The poverty the hu-
mility does not prevent your
        repeat

130

Divinity As for me
I weep for it The poverty and the hu-
mility of your love are
certain proofs As for
me I weep   my good
God sobbing I present
to you the myrrh (of the
marriages)   As for me
to think of it I am more dead
than alive A day for
us on a cross of
organists   -   As   mortal
without radio from the royal
biographer
you take our miseries
You must die for the
salvation of all-[listening
to their organ concerts-
of Children here is the fête of Noël
It is the New Year for pleasure
each one prepares himself Look what
élan the winter has on : nature has
Imperial
thrown off its manteau . No more
flowers no more verdure And
this husband of Ermine
all the same it's beautiful.....
Midnight Christians it is
the solemn hour ... as in
days of old a shining star

lead there the Magis from the Orient
Mistral and Mirielle su
ite spanish Toreros
We are in April the
meadows turn green the almond
trees cover themselves in white and
rose flowers -. the-
Alps like a pedestal of
gilded granite in the blue sky =
its human floes face of
like
Napoleon risen on earth. the
astonished people could but fall
quiet Arms raised he presented
to the earth |when shall I have it all
flourished| his newly born child
One would speak the Welkerschlacht
or the pedestal of the Siegesalle
calm
like a mysterious gliding beacon
in the heavens Mme de Staël
danced around like a
Liberty fallen from the Welkerschl-
lacht - panier full of almond
tree roses the helmet lantern
of crimson and gold at twilight
the grand Campeador.
general disarmament (remains a
revue of banquets and bouquets final

take as Joan of Arc nude in
(modern
the red Catherine on a horse
the cords of the banner of
brocade . throughout
the long folds dragging along in corona
tion banners - Like
a belt of vivid crimson of He-
rod laced in ribbons of the 7 natural of the ancient wo-
rld rolling within at its feet
the organist and his book of Operas
where these 7 Wonders in natural romance
novel + appear on the oeuvres of Gou-
on the Bible of Larousse
nod composer : Mireille . Sapho
Faust . Romeo and Juliette Philemon
and Baucis (The Illumination of the creation by
the city of Lights of Broadway --
Return Jerusalem all illuminated like Picadilly - the city of the
roses - Copenhagen. Ouchy bouquet of
Bengal fireworks. the novel
of the rose Hymn to Marie or
of Gounod
Ave - Maria di lampe de
Veneti the pope in his manteau The
swing
queen of Carthage the queen of
Saba the queen Esther-Jesabel
The daughter of the Pharoah   The Queen Victoria
the rose in diadems   -   The Empress Eli-

133

sabeth - The Empress Eugenie - and
her necklace of Castles of Queen Berthe Opera Sphinx Victoria
- Cleopatra - Iphigénie
at Aulis a sirena
at the edge of the blue nile a
true balustrade in necklace of the
Capitol _ The Composer Gounod _ Romeo and Juliette -
Faust his necklace of pink pearls
of India Sappho and her bouquet
on the bed of orange flowers-
Werther marriage in the auto bou
quet of orchids of Pregny Rosia -
Gaynlmiter Wilhelm II
Iphigenia at Aulis
several ballets and the opera singer
one throws some flowers here
Jenny Lindt _ Walkyria
Ave Maria - 6 airs -
Mme Lohengrin Zita
remains at the feet with her
vessel as a wedding basket
he has
fallen in her long manteau
in abducting her to a luxuriously
furnished grotto -
disembarking from Kythira
flames of angel Gambetta

blond in the arms of the general
of high command kneeling__She
too had the air of an angel of
white marble of the   Easter
processions in Spain
them as white eagle very lofty
like the sails of a boat of
butcher painter-the air still
of a flame of the wond-
-ers of the world in
her   nuptial sails____in
her Imperial manteau
Madame de Staël   (the universe
it is hers Space your present
Napoleon remembers her _
Delphine Corinne of
·Germany - the angel is found
in the name Charlemagne
7 crowns
and his numismatic mad-
of the 7 wonders of the ancient world
onnas - a great Eu
ropean - and his gigan-
tic crimson velarium at
Versailles-French Russian and Vau
dois at Caux. on the palace of the Krem-
lin Alexandra _ on the Palace of Ru-
has the air of an ice floe that erects itself in Egypt
mine is covered in a coronation
of banners and the giant

of Thule sinks in the sea carriage

flags in 13 red banners
and 48 extremely pointed stars
of the Capital explode (or exploding) in the
wind of Atlantis . its por-
ticos of elephants or the mahad
rajah descends from the height of his throne
of Dheli many pachyderms laying
down under the roma and
erect themselves in bronze launching
into the space the floats of victory and
its golden suspended lamp in
the banners of Chinese azure
the sphinx of the Siangelée-ey)
painted inside in garlanding
Bonaparte and his heraldic carriages
helvetic flowers flourishes
on the manteau of the Empr
ess Elizabeth [in the Larousse]
on the altar of the Swiss homeland at
Montre/ux) of gold vineyards plan
ted in flowers of archangels of Saint
Légier walk like a swan and
silver cup an angel lily-
pad of its wings in the air this incom-
of angsoka
parable flower [marble the winter settling
upon the vessel of the Bible of
nature composing the coffers of the

How well you take   - this green cup - of the cup of

multicolored monuments
carriage of the Bon Enfant the engagement
coffers of the Mahadrajah
necklace of pink pearls of India (Bazar
Béchert) the engagement carriage
of the engagement carriages of the
parade floats of psyche of the palan-
quins of the Spanish Béatrice
                    d'Este
carried the day of Easter of <u>Oté
ro</u> [jewels of terrelita of Mario Medicis
the museums of ydillic painting of
nature. She has her Sédia or a
portable bed. The sorceresse at the balcony
of the ampitheater of the temples of
Jupiter -- or on the sea Triton -
in his manteau rolls her
golden book of the Creation - under
the kiss of the Sun $\underline{as\,a}$ Resplendent Lord of the li-
ght has stretched out the sky li
ke a carpet on his adored
          in the bed of the roses
feet. each page would o-
pen itself the torn manteau of
Bonaparte; gushing then the bou
quets or jets of water of flowers of lig
ht Bengalese fireworks of Sans Souci
all the Siegesallees Colonnaded
around the <u>World map </u>flower

natural

Vessel many

azure

of

cup

as

like a bouquet of flower of
light Magnificent unity
magic
light (of Broadway) and pu-
rity it's a ray of flowers
(organs) cry of calling to the heart
saintliness saintliness
Sacrificed beauty it is like
a song of the flowers
charity charity by MC.
Chrysanthemum- in music
little Geisha chrysanthemum with
multiple and changing sweet little faces
that crown with a diadem
the Japanese and the Chinese of
crimson and of gold always coiffed
for the pleasure of the Mikado offering her tousled nape out of some
adorable Kimono (-in ô dove
immolated on the altar or the flowered
bank of Lygie) and her Ursus-the wind
of the seas blows from Asia on your
jagged plumes and confers
to their frenzy an ephemeral
royalty. For you brandish on the
pale winter the flowering scepter
of your disdain And die in
beauty last love of the
garden-by Isabelle Kaiser in

other words all the earth flourishes under the flowered scepter of renovation in love dress that
one puts on the earth in adoration always. God is the name that all
adore when the summit turns golden and
covers it with the manteau sparkling with <u>verdure</u> and life.

The tallying of Bethlehem
and the escape in Egypt = An
angel (appeared in dream of the Lord
to Joseph and said to him raise up
take the little child and his mother
escape to Egypt . Matthew
<u>2-13 painting of Fra Angelico</u>

Of the Creator all repeat the power
his name <u>fills</u> the universe in singing it nature incenses it mor
tal listen to its concerts To the firmament
God drives the stars God sheds
the rays of the day Of the somber night
he rends the veils to brighten it
with his love - to brighten it
with his love - repeat At the heart of the
waves eternal harmonies unite the voice
of the vast heavens to celebrate its infinite power in mysterious accents
the haughty oak the fragile herb
sprig are the slaves of his law And his
Justice in breaking the superb raise up
the humble by his faith raise up the humble
by his faith -

This Imperial crown flower
astral of charity flourishes in bedding
of the   car
imperial under the flowered sc
        sumptuous hierophant of the
epter of renovation when the stars
        seasons arises in bronze
write the name of the Lord God
        on the 7 wonders of the
in bowing their corollas of fire
        natural world
or their crowns of fire since
        of fire
the ocean carriage of the Gau
risancar . dragging the nuptial

veils on the Mont Blanc
        his Marie Louise
covers Napoleon with tiara stoles
or the Liberty of America   dan
cing with the Emperor / so sings
and dances America in music)
all her cotillions that she picks up
        the Liberty
on the nature (in flower gets bogged
        the Malibran
down in the Léman d'Azur and
I saw her blush like the
rosvelt (like Schwilge as
one likes it) and of the love to
embellish herself She was traversing Eu
rope a harp attached to her heart
                organs   the
She lingered in Her Carriage the peoples
        7 wonders of the anciet world
transported in her arms - Let us
stay united like a bouquet

of flowers The call of the flowers ô in
the adversity let us stay well united

Quo vadis = (Domine)

where do you go Lord, God
I saw flourish your beautiful
heaven of Italy and your rose-
winged sirens of   Lotus   o n
the bank of Lygie crown
ed in your arms [in dress
of love with which one covers the
earth (in adoring it always
       royal
God is the name that all
adore when the peak gilds itself
             Cimarosa
in its manteau sparkling of
on its throne of 7 candelabras 7 wonders of the world
verdure and of life) as

Ô Dove im –
molated on the altar

on the stage the Venus de Milo of
the theater fête has tainted as sor-
ceress her royal court manteau
of the diadem of the Savior her dress
of butterfly of paphos - of lily-
pads____in the bed of the roses
to kiss the marble statues
in toilette de Venus_ remains the mon
ument of Jupiter in the garlands
of psyche roses hurled at him
She throws some flowers in his face.

act 1   ô Palés   la Fête des Vignerons

The spring Zephyr rekindles the verdure the divine nightingale on the
young branches repeats his hymn
to nature And alerts it
shepherd tired from his rest in the beloved
pasture redirects his herds
Palès deity of the prairies spreads upon
the rivers flowered by your new
presents a fragrant treasure. Dress
in your colors and the mounts and
On the silk reed and in the fields along
the plains gush forth tremendously
the tranquil lake all reflected
the crystal of the fountains--
generously the smile of the heavens
Give the breeze a sweet rise
And the bird a more agile impulse _ _ _ =
Alongside the tranquil lake
[And the angels] are the smile of the heavens
= The primrose bursts in gracious
bouquets The primrose bursts
in bouquets in gracious
bouquets- ô Bacchus -Solo-
ô Bacchus . ô Bacchus   ô Bacchus
ô Cérès you garland the altar
of nature. [in your arms] Grey Book
the suite of Soli = The violet of Schiller --- The earth is his work / Jupiter
is his share / the Creator /
appears on his hand

BILLET À L'INCONNUE
23 mai 1947

Sous les arbres de grand abri
de Paris
en on est parties en tant!
rêve en train de pour pré
Paris G.S. rêve de paradis de chef
nous porter nos
dans les bras les pieds nus
les pierre lunes
continue perles
de l'Inde de toutes
lunes sur le port de
perles de grand perles la tête
à Napoléon volée
sur son cocarde la Madone de France
Corse jolie

BILLET à L'INCONNUE

23 mai 1947.

Gérard Saint-Clair

145

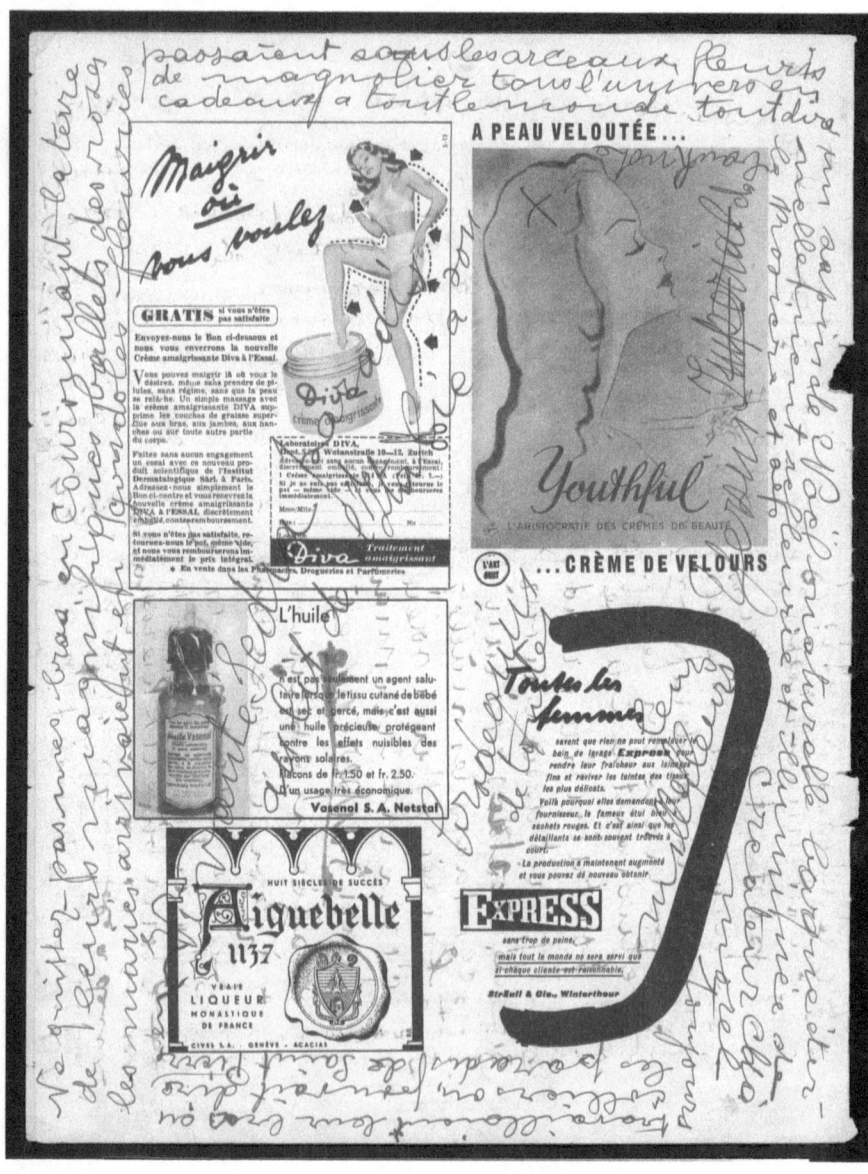

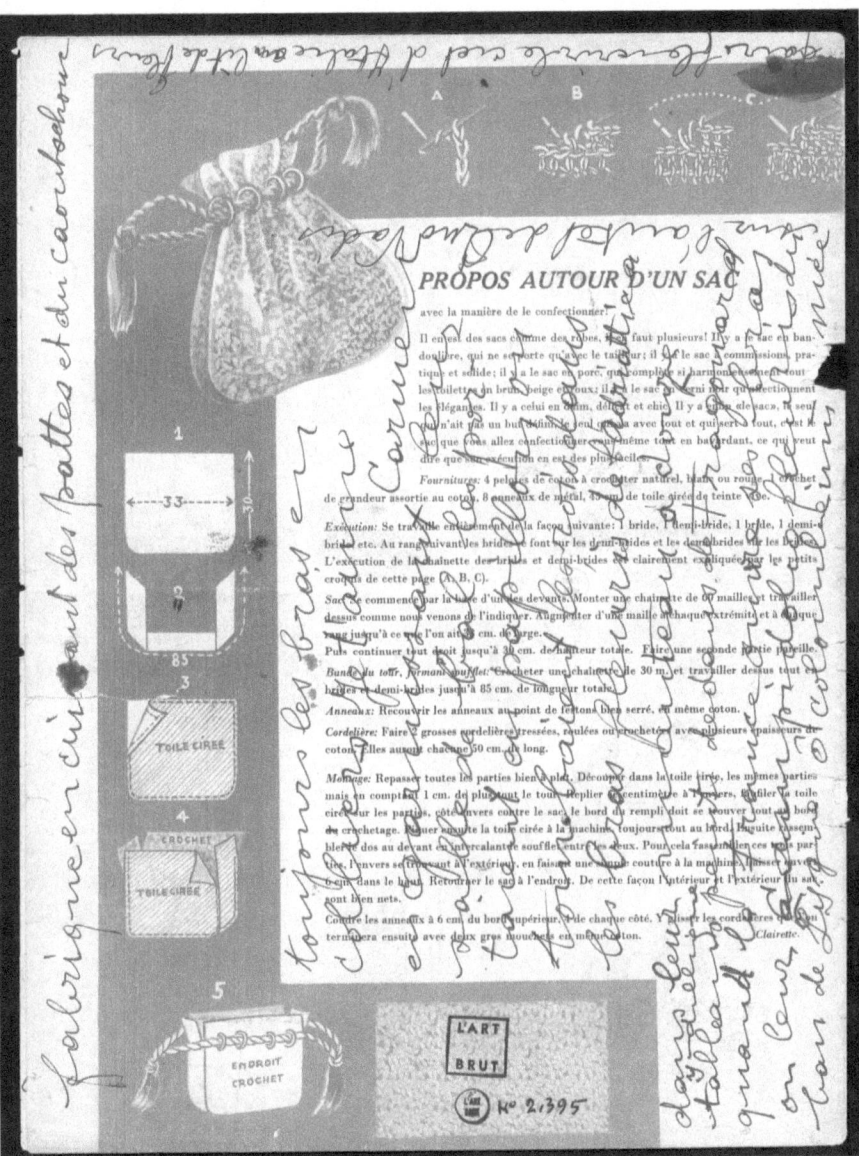

LETTER TO ANONYMOUS
23 May 1947

Under the trees of the great   refuge

of Paris   carriage

    we left   by

in   a dream in train of crim son -s

   dream of paradise of

Paris   to bring us our   chiefs

in the arms barefooted   on

the stone   moon honey

continuous   pearls pink

of India   of all co

lors on   the port of

pearls of great   price the head

of Napoleon   flight

on his heart, the Madonna of France

Corsica pretty isle of love one

earth adores on their
roman chariots of Tepsis
carry in their
arms their sirens
in white of the Ri-
ponne where the
student de Gaule
make thus the great
bridge of loves
of the king of kings thr
ust into the thousand
fuses of a sun
like a man
Imperial in
terwoven in sphinx
Promethean
their arms one car-
ried from immense
esumuous hieroglyphant
only hundreds of bouquets
that one contemplates in pairs
dent who carries his tableau
could say in this crowd the stu

rightly ó the Matadors that all the
floats advance by the thousands up-
of flowers in battalions of flowers that the Parade

149

passed beneath the flowered archways
of the magnolia trees all the universe as
presents to everyone tell everything

bankote

Do not leave my arms in crowning the earth
of their magnificent rose ballets
the married arrive in flowered gondolas
in

Living Sedia paradise
in the bed of Italy
has his

brodequin
of all

a Christmas tree natural small boat eternally reflowering and illuminated
the Rosière and its

Imperial

Yersey Sunrise

Creator Cha
morel

their
millefleurs

working their arms in
necklace one could say
the heavens of Saint Pierre

150

fabricate by cooking some hooves and some rubber

always arms in
necklaces I love you
in garnishing their Carmen
ball room brought
them some butterfly where
the kings fell into
the flowered arms of the Adriatica
in their manteau of twelve
painting
painted tableau of Fragonard
when France opens its arms
where their flowered Campidolio of
Lygie ban Ô dove immo lated

on the altar of Quo Vadis

to make flower the sky of Italy in the bed of flowers

CRYPTOPHASIC IDIOGLOSSIA: LEXICON

To fall in love with words, one forms a language around them. To fixate on an image, one forms a way of seeing around it. To obsess over a theory, rational or not, is to redirect one's course through life. As the fantasy takes on its own life within the self, one refers to it in shorthand, through symbols or metonym. The process of appropriating and personalizing renews and enhances the meaning of that embezzled cultural referent. While it is impossible to divine the specific significance Aloïse attached to each term addressed in the following lexicon, the definitions are intended to provide a reference to their common meanings. Where possible, their meaning specific to the text is also defined.

ALOÏSE'S UNIVERSE: FOUNDATION WORDS

Drawing on Jacqueline Porret-Forel's (JPF) reading of Aloïse's terminology in La Voleuse de Mappemonde *and offering alternative definitions, this first set of definitions describes the central terms of Aloïse's universe. These elements appear throughout her work.*

Consubstantialité Alternative (*Alternative Consubstantiality*)

"Consubstantiality" describes the relationship of the Divine beings of the Christian Trinity, who take different forms but share a single essence. In Aloïse's Alternative Consubstantiality, the tripartite entity is formed of personages from her life; as creator of her universe and its essence, she is each of these personages and embodies consubstantiality, or being-in-multiple.

[*See also: La Terre; Trinitaries*]

Église Universel (*Universal Church*)

1. According to JPF, the term "Universal Church" represents madness in Aloïse's drawings and writings. One could read "madness," *la folie*, as rapture or as transfiguration of the mind and spirit. 2. Read literally, "Universal Church" could also reference the Christian or Catholic Church, or the spirituality inherent in all things.

[*See also: Pierre*]

Lulu

Aloïse renamed herself Lulu when, interned at Clery, she relinquished her past self and its connection to what she called the "ancient world of other-times." The birth of the Lulu persona marked a resigned letting-go of an entire lived history and the abandonment of the possibility of its natural progression into the future. As Lulu, Aloïse is reborn as her own universe—the Earth—and becomes the entity governing it. Within this universe, Lulu's main avatars are "the royal earth;" "the Creator *Bon-Enfant* (Christ-Child);" and "the Prisoner Queen" (represented by Marie

Stuart or Anne Boleyn). Minor avatars assume the form of the Pope, the Sphinx, and the Siren.

[*See also:* Alternative Consubstantiality; Marie Stuart; Promethean Sphinx; Ricochet Solaire; La Terre; Transfiguration; Trinitaries]

Psalm 104 de Humboldt (*Humbolt's Psalm 104*)

Aloïse memorized an astonishing number of Biblical verses by heart. The exquisitely rendered imagery of Psalm 104 must have been firmly imprinted on Aloïse's consciousness; she makes direct reference to the hymn in her writings and drawings. A simultaneously sorrowful and joyous hymn exalting the magnificence of God's creation, this psalm is thought by some to be "Adam's song," lamenting his expulsion from the Garden of Eden. The following is excerpted from Psalm 104 1:6:

> *Praise the LORD, O my soul. O LORD my God, you*
> *are very great; you are clothed with splendor and majesty.*
> *He wraps himself in light as with a garment; he*
> *stretches out the heavens like a tent*
> *and lays the beams of his upper chambers on their*
> *waters. He makes the clouds his chariot and rides on*
> *the wings of the wind.*
> *He makes wind his messengers, flames of fire his servants.*
> *He set the earth on its foundations; it can never be moved.*
> *You covered it with the deep as with a garment; the*
> *waters stood above the mountains.*

Alexander von Humboldt, a 19th century explorer, scientist, and author of *Cosmos* and *Personal Narrative of Travels to the Equinoctial Regions of the New Continent During the Years 1799–1804*, wrote of Psalm 104:

> *It might almost be said that this one Psalm represents*
> *the image of the whole Cosmos. We are astonished to*
> *find in a lyrical poem of such a limited compass, the*
> *whole universe—the heavens and the earth—sketched*
> *with a few bold touches. The calm and toilsome labor*
> *of man, from the rising of the sun to the setting of the*
> *same, when his daily work is done, is here contrasted*

with the moving life of the elements of nature. This contrast and generalization in the conception of the mutual action of natural phenomena, and this retrospection of an omnipresent invisible power, which can renew the earth or crumble it to dust, constitute a solemn and exalted rather than a glowing and gentle form of poetic creation.

"LE SACRE DE NAPOLÉON" ("THE CORONATION OF NAPOLEON")

One of Aloïse's primary fixations was a painting entitled *"Le Sacre de Napoléon."* Completed in 1807 by Jacques-Louis David, it supplied her with a vast wealth of imagery and narrative. At 10×6 meters, sited in Notre Dame Cathedral, the painting seems to merge into the cathedral's cavernous depth. Upon visiting Le Sacre in David's atelier, Napoleon quipped, "it is not a painting, one *walks through* this tableaux." JPF wrote that Le Sacre must have appeared to Aloïse almost like a comic strip, the various scenes unfolding within the whole to open worlds of possibilities.

Both people and objects from this painting populate Aloïse's universe, a testament to David's preoccupation with accurately rendering the portraits of each dignitary and accounting for the many splendid accessories of the imperial regalia. The cast of the massive opus includes all those within sight of the Coronation—those looking on from the balconies and those in the procession itself: Napoleon Bonaparte, Josephine, Talleyrand (thinker and lover of Germaine de Staël), Joachim Murat (King of Naples), Jacques Louis David and family, and Pope Pius VII. David also depicts the objects presented to the Emperor and the Pope for the purpose of guaranteeing their sacredness: The Hand of Justice, The Imperial Globe, The Imperial Scepter, The Epée of Charlemagne "Joyeuse," The Crown of Charlemagne, and the Scepter of Charles V.

If Le Sacre furnishes Aloïse's universe of fabulous things and god-like persons, text from Frederic Masson's 1911 account of the coronation, *Napoleon and His Coronation* (1911) also seems to find its way into her writing. Masson's description includes a full detail of each article of clothing, including the origin of the material, the cost, and when possible the name of the artisan. Josephine and Napoleon don the decadent and heavy *grand tapis*, a manteau of crimson and ermine, embroidered with golden bees (the Napoleonic symbol). Both costumes are of white silk and satin embroidered with gold and silver. Napoleon's open crown is formed of golden olive tree leaves, and Josephine's diadem of pearls is enriched with gold and precious stones. The pope wore, by imperial decree, a cape of gold and silver embroidered with flowers, a lace trimmed surplice, a silver cloth tiara, three golden-hoop-crowns, and a cross of gold studded with diamonds, pearls, and colored stones. The fact that every costume detail of each echelon of imperial rank is *prescribed* is as astounding as the astronomical expenditures recorded—3,345 precious stones and 2,990 pearls were employed in the creation of the imperial wardrobes.

[*See also:* Coppet; Hermine; La Malibran; Manteau; Napoleon Bonaparte; Pierre; Trinitaries]

RICOCHET SOLAIRE (*SOLAR RICOCHET*)

The Solar Ricochet brings light and breathes life into a dead Earth. It is a catalyst within Aloïse's work and the inspiration for her creation. If one imagines Aloïse bathed in the light shining from the Ricochet Solaire, one would see images literally springing forth from her imagination, evincing new life springing forth as well. Aloïse describes it as follows: "*That sleeping earth, inert, is awakened by the grand celestial bell with its stars, fertilized by the touch of the sun's rays that fall upon it and cause it to spout forth in ricochet, a multitude of images ... immortally famished in the night beneath the triple astral bouquet, tree of life, that fuses the flesh of an golden earthen urn of caressed with a dash of Passion of the celestial Plows of the flowers of its body which it sows.*"[Porret-Forel, Jacqueline. *Aloïse et le théâtre de l'univers* (Genève: Éditions d'Art Albert Skira,1993) p. 104.]

One must read the Solar Ricochet as an action performed upon the personages, the artist, and the earth with its many splendid things. This action causes the transformation of all things caught in its rays. In Foucauldian terms, the Solar Ricochet makes all things visible, and thereby knowable, by shining light upon them.

The Solar Ricochet both unveils the newly born world and brings life to things themselves by making them available to knowledge.

[*See also:* Transfiguration]

LA TERRE (*THE EARTH*)

Aloïse is first reincarnated as earth itself, as mud, as dust, having lost the breath of life—having lost her self of the ancient world of other times—and become completely extinguished. In becoming the earth, Aloïse begins re-conceptualizing all human existence. She is reborn through God's providence as the first human and the first woman. In this first period, she refers to herself as "Lulu," signing her writings with this name. Later, Aloïse is reborn again as the capital-E Earth, the home and the foundation of all humankind. In her terms, she is the *world-map* or the *royal earth thrown into space*. In this second formation (which is a significant aspect of her later texts and drawings), she assumes a generative function blossoming with life, and catalyzing new growth.

[*See also:* Lulu]

TRANSFIGURATION

Transfiguration refers to Christ's visible glorification in the presence of three of his disciples (Matthew 17:2, Mark 9:2, Luke 9:28-36). In the scripture is written that his face glowed as if of the sun, and his "raiment was white as light," or perhaps it was as though he were kissed by the Solar Ricochet. Transfiguration more generally implies a transformative process through which a higher state of being is attained. In Aloïse's oeuvre, this refers to the filter that processes all things from the "ancient world of other times" as they are born into her universe.

Like many schizophrenics, Aloïse adored artifice and disdained artifacts reminiscent of the real world. She preferred those things that were already filtered, already removed from nature. She cared very little for actual flowers for instance, save for their utilitarian purpose of providing pigments for drawings. As her eidetic memory provided an unfathomably rich source of imagery from which to cull, many of the places and people in her work can be directly traced back to specific artworks, advertisements, or texts.

It's likely that her sources are the reproduced or altered images rather than the actual sites, as again, Aloïse was fascinated with that which was already removed from nature.

The object of Aloïse's word play was the transfiguration of language. This was not a game, but a rather serious neologistic task of transforming a language to meet her unique demands. It was also a self-defensive strategy: she created a universe anew and possessed its only key; she created language anew and became its sole mediate being.

[*See also:* Post Tenebras Lux; Ricochet Solaire; Transfiguration of Rapahel]

TRINITARIES

The personages of the Trinity only appear in Aloïse's earlier writings. In later texts, their works and existence are implied and their presence is felt rather than directly illustrated. These trinitaries direct Aloïse's destiny and offer her protection. Though they exist apart from her, they are also of her flesh and blood. The original trinitaries are personalities who, for one reason or another, Aloïse held in very high regard. "Dominant personages, their own existence had only been perceived by her in an imaginary world. These violent passions for an 'inaccessible man whom I love infinitely,' could only result in repeated failures." [Porret-Forel, Jacqueline, *La Voleuse de Mappemonde: Les écrits d'Aloïse.* (Genève: Éditions Zoé, 2004) p. 30.]

P. Gabriel Chamorel
An artist and professor of theology in Lausanne who participated in workers' strikes.

[*See also:* Porret-Forel, Jacqueline, *La Voleuse de Mappemonde: Les écrits d'Aloïse.* (Genève: Éditions Zoé, 2004) p. 30.]

Albert Mahaim
The chief doctor at Cery hospital, where Aloïse was interned.

[*See also:* Marguerite]

GUILLAUME II

His Imperial and Royal Majesty Wilhelm the Second, by the Grace of God, German Emperor and King of Prussia, descended of the House of Hohenzollern. It is possible that Aloïse once caught sight of Guillaume II (or Kaiser Wilhelm II) during her residence in Pottsdam, though it is highly unlikely that the two ever met. The emperor was a source of much heartache and romanticizing—Aloïse's love of the fabulously regal world of the European aristocracy drove her to delve into romantic fantasies for the Kaiser, though Guillaume was not the most attractive of men. He suffered from mental illness, was born with a withered left arm, and was often criticized for his megalomaniacal tendencies. His reign marked the end of the German monarchy.

[*See also:* L'Achilleion; Dryander; Henninke; *Sans Souci;* Siegesallee]

NAPOLEON BONAPARTE

Infamous emperor who recurs throughout Aloïse's oeuvre. In her work he most often appears in relation to other notable figures.

[*See also:* Le Sacre de Napoléon; Lulu; Saint Esprit; Walewska at Finkenstein]

ALOÏSE'S UNIVERSE: INDUCTIVE WORDS

*JPF terms "inductive words" those that have multiple implications and illu-
minate many significations. Though these seem disordered in Aloïse's work,
they are in fact ordered according to a very rigorous system. "To decrypt the
inductive words," she writes, "one must take into account:*

> *Their diverse exceptions*
> *Their systematic linkage to other words*
> *The mental associations and evocations that they provoke*
> *Their symbolic power*
> *And certainly the assonances that generate other series
> of words."*

L'ACHILLEION

In 1907 Kaiser Wilhelm II purchased a hillside villa on the isle of
Corfu that had been the vacation home of the Empress Elizabeth
of Hapsburg. Purchased as a fixer-upper of sorts, the site (like
Greece as a whole) was initially of interest to the Kaiser because
of his fascination with archaeology, religion and mythology.
Unfortunately for him, the great relics unearthed on his property
during his special archaeological digs had been planted there in
his absence by the Greek help. One of his great finds was a bas-
relief bearing likeness to one of the Gorgons. The villa is named
for the Greek god Achilles, portraits and sculptures of whom are
found throughout the interior and surrounding gardens. At one
point Kaiser Wilhelm II ordered the removal of a statue of Jewish
lyricist Heinrich Heine from the property; Ernest Herter's *Dying
Achilles* was then commissioned for the garden.

[*See also:* Christomanos; Guillaume II; Hôtel de Caux, Iphigenia at
Aulis; Trinitaries]

BOUQUET

1. Aloïsian bouquets appear in the standard form associated
with the word (a grouping or arrangement of flowers) but also
as explosive groupings of stars, artificial lights, specific flowers,
water fountains, butterflies, diamonds, and astral forms, among
others. 2. Like the *manteau*, the form of the bouquet also implies
an action—a bursting forth of life and of substance. *Bouquet final,*
the finale of a fireworks display, marks the apex of excitement or

intensities. *"Donner un bouquet à quelqu'un"* (to give a bouquet to someone) is a figure of speech meaning to offer a warm welcome or a favor.

[*See also:* Manteau; Marguerite; Ricochet Solaire]

HERMINE

1. *Hermine* translates to ermine or stoat stole; in Aloïse's work it implies the elegance and luxuriousness associated with such finery. Ermine appears more frequently in the drawings than the texts and is symbolic of prestige and royalty, but also of femininity. 2. Hermine is also a surname and Saint-Hermine is a French commune in the Loire valley. 3. "Hermine" appearing in the text operates much like the words *pourpre, nacre,* and *doré* (crimson, mother-of-pearl, and gilt).

[*See also:* Le Sacre de Napoléon]

MANTEAU

1. A direct translation of the word *manteau* is "overcoat" or "mantle." 2. Taking into account the functions of providing warmth, protection, and concealment, the Aloïsian manteau could also be read as delimiting interior and exterior space. 3. The phrase *"sous le manteau"* means to execute something clandestinely and could be understood in relation to female sexuality and metamorphosis. *"Il ne s'est pas fait déchirer le manteau"* (he did not tear his coat) is a figure of speech describing someone who isn't taken to prayer. *"Garder les manteaux"* (to keep the coats on) means to be secreted or private. 4. Josephine and Napoleon Bonaparte's coronation manteaux were crimson in color and lined with fur. Aloïse often strings together manteau + imperial/royal + crimson + other terms denoting the majestic. 5. The manteau is often found in simile (something spreads like a manteau) or enacts a specific function (it serves as a tableau for illustration or reveals what is hidden).

[*See also:* Bouquet, Le Sacre de Napoléon]

MARGUERITE

1. In Aloïse' life there were many women named Marguerite. Those most noteworthy include her eldest sister, who sternly took

charge of the Corbaz household following their mother's early death, and who also suffered mental illness later in life; Madame Marguerite Mahaim, wife of Professor Mahaim; and Madame Marguerite Muller, wife of Doctor C. Muller of the Rosière. 2. Margaret of Bourgogne of the "Tour de Nesles" scandal was one of two sisters accused by their family of adultery and sentenced to life imprisonment. 3. There are at least a dozen saints and well-known martyrs named Marguerite. 4. Marguerite translates to "daisy" in English. The game *he loves me, he loves me not,* is generally associated with daisies (in French this is called *effeuiller la marguerite*). As it produces on average an excess of two-dozen petals, it is in itself a sort of self-contained *bouquet final* (a fireworks finale).

[*See also:* Bouquet; Trinitaries; Denantour de Nesles; Gounod; La Traviata; Mahaim; Trinitaries]

Pierre/pierre

1. A *pierre* is a stone, a rock, or something upon which to build a construction, or out of which to carve a sculpture; in all cases it is earthen material made rare by its density. As raw material it invites transformation—through artistry or construction—into an alternate form. In Aloïse's universe, stones also appear as precious stones: diamonds, sapphires, and so on. 2. Saint Peter: *Pierre* is the French equivalent of "Peter." Saint Peter was one of the three apostles to witness the Transfiguration of Christ. He was the Christ-Appointed Head of the Apostles, and his missionary tour ended in martyrdom. Originally called Simon, Peter was given the name "Cephas" following his profession of faith in Christ. In the book of Matthew it is recounted that Jesus told Simon that his new name, Peter, could be interpreted as "Kephas." Kephas, Kipha (Aramaiac), petro, or petra, means pebble, boulder, or rock; Peter is figuratively the rock upon which the Christian church was built. 3. *Pierrot:* A pierrot is a clown, a sparrow, or a Frenchman. 4. *Père:* Père means father in the holy sense, the familial sense, and in relation to Père Noël (Father Christmas).

[*See also:* Jean-Pierre Calloc'h; Le Sacre; Pierre Chanlaine; Pierrefontaine; Saint-Pierre; Transfiguration; Universal Church]

Sans-souci translates to "carefree." It is the name of the royal château of Frederic II of Prussia, Schloss Sans-Souci. Completed in 1748, Sans-Souci was to be the royal get-away from the stresses of aristocratic life in Berlin. After the death of Frederic II, the palace became the property of Kaiser Wilhelm II. The palace is often compared to Versailles and is constructed and decorated in Rococo style. It was intended to appear light and airy.

[*See also:* Guillaume II; Pierrefontaine]

UNCOMMON FIGURES

A lexicon of uncommon figures appearing in each translation. Texts are in chronological order, with figures in order of appearance in each text.

LETTRE À GUILLAUME II / LETTER TO GUILLAUME II
28 April 1917

MONSIEUR DE COPPET EX PRESIDENT OF THE SWISS CONFEDERATION

1. The Monsieur de Coppet of Aloïse's "Letter to Guillaume II" is most likely Jacques Necker, Louis XVI's finance minister and father of Madame Germaine de Staël, organizer of the circle of intellectuals known as the "Coppet Group." 2. de Coppet might also refer to Jules Marcel de Coppet, French governor of West African colonies. He is noteworthy for fighting colonial abuses, for encouraging André Gide to write *Voyage au Congo,* and for authoring French colonial policies. However, most of his work was done after "Letter to Guillaume II" was written; at the time of its writing he was known only as an influential intellectual.

[*See also:* Bernadin de Saint Pierre; Chateau de Montaulieu; Coppet; Kervadec]

SAINT-ESPRIT

1. Marie de la Charité du Saint-Esprit, née Marie-Josèphe-Caroline Brader, was born in St. Gallen, Switzerland in 1860. She was the founder of the Congregation of the Franciscan Sisters of Marie Immaculate. 2. Saint-Esprit may also refer to one of the many congregations or hospitals of that name. 3. More simply, and most probably, Saint-Esprit is The Holy Ghost, a direct translation from English.

[*See also:* Trinitaries]

LE GRAND HORLOGER (*THE GREAT CLOCKMAKER*)

The clockmaker appears in René Descartes' *Méditations métaphysiques* as a concept metaphor illustrating his arguments for natural theology and the knowledge and acceptance of God through reason. If all the universe is an intricate machine, it must surely have been created by some being possessing knowledge of its inner-workings.

> « L'univers m'embarrasse, et je ne puis songer
> Que cette horloge existe et n'ait point d'horloger. »

> ["The universe confounds me, and I cannot dream
> That this clock exists and yet has no clockmaker."]

> — Voltaire, Les Cabales, 1772

[*See also:* Zaïra]

LA GRANDE MADONNE À VALLOTTON / THE GREAT MADONNA OF VALLOTTON
25 *March 1920*

THE TRANSFIGURATION OF RAPHAEL
Raphael (Raffaello Sanzio) was commissioned by Pope Clement VII in 1515 to paint a portrayal of the transfiguration of Christ. The immense *Transfiguration* was donated to the church of San Pietro in Montorio following Raphael's death; transported to Paris during the Napoleonic Era; and eventually returned to Italy. It is considered to be Raphael's last painting.

[*See also:* The Burning of Balthazar; Transfiguration]

CHIESA OF THE SAINT FATHER BENOÎT XV
Chiesa is Italian for "church." This *chiesa* is the church of Saint Benoît XV, also known as Pope Benedict XV, born Giacomo Paolo Giovanni Battista della Chiesa. Benedict XV was pope from 1914–1922. During the First World War he issued a Plea for Peace, demanding the cessation of hostile acts and calling for international arbitration. The only national leader to respond to his call for peace was United States President Woodrow Wilson, who replied that at the current time peace was impossible. In the end,

Wilson did enact some of the peace-making proposals laid out by the Pope.

[*See also:* St. Légier]

THE PRINCE OF PEACE 1914-1920

William II or Kaiser Wilhelm II or Guillaume II was also called the "prince of peace."

[*See also:* Sans-Souci; Trinitaries]

THE ASTRONOMER VETTER

This is most likely Alois Rudolph Vetter, a German pathological anatomist. His publications were the first of their kind in German and were influenced by those of Marie François Xavier Bichat, who is best known for identifying tissues as distinct forms separate within the human body. Aloïse mentions Vetter in another text, "*Lettre sur Papier Étroit,*" followed by the quote "*omnis cellula e cellula.*" Translated literally, this means "where a cell arises, there a cell must previously have been" and is a theory developed by Rudolph Virchow describing how the fissioning of cells forms new life. That astronomer and anatomist are perhaps purposely confused illustrates Aloïse's interest in and liberal application of their philosophies.

LE NOËL DE SAINT-ROSAIRE / NOËL OF SAINT-ROSAIRE

c. 1921

WALTER SCOTT

Scott is a Scottish poet and novelist (1771–1832), best known for *Ivanhoe, Guy Mannering,* and *Rob Roy.* He also authored a controversial account of Napoleon Bonaparte's life, entitled *The Life of Napoleon Buonaparte, Emperor of the French* (1827), which would certainly have been of interest to Aloïse. Scott also visited Lausanne in 1826, after the Château Chillon of Montreux and its environs were romanticized in Lord Byron's writings.

[*See also:* The Intuition of Byron]

Fritz Heim
Heim was a professor at the University of Lausanne.

[*See also:* Vallaton Paul Bridel and Saillens]

Evangel of Eplattenier
1. Charles l'Éplattenier, Swiss painter and Art Nouveau artist, most famous for his having taught Le Corbusier, would be the simplest association. 2. "Evangel of Eplattenier" also points to another Charles l'Éplattenier and a Jean-Louis Éplattenier who were pastors in Switzerland, but their writings are dated well after 1921. 3. There must have been a lesser-known Éplattenier associated with the church.

Félix Faure
Faure was the president of France from 1895–1899.

Cordilliaries
Cordilleras are mountain ranges running along a coastline.

[*See also:* Popocatepetl]

Gaurisankar
The second highest peak in the Himalayas, the name of which means "the Goddess Shiva and her Consort" in Sanskrit, was originally mistaken for Mount Everest because of their proximity and apparent similarity from a distance.

Holy War in 1912
The "Holy War of 1912" is the name given to the First Balkan War, in which the Balkan League (including Bulgaria, Montenegro, Greece, and Serbia) went to war against the Ottoman Empire. Although this dispute officially ended in 1913, the Second Balkan War began the same year.

[*See also:* Ismet Pacha]

The three hills of Lausanne
The city of Lausanne is nestled amidst three hills: La Cité, Le Bourg, and Saint-Laurent.

PÉNÉLOPE FABRIC TERRESTRIAL ENVELOPE

Penelope, the wife of Odysseus in Homer's *Odyssey*, waits for her husband's return for 20 years while he fights in the Trojan War and travels home. During this time, she fends off suitors in various ways, one of the most fantastic of which is her never-ending weaving of a burial shroud for her father (she weaves by day and partially unravels at night). She promises she will consider marriage to another man when this endless task is complete. *"C'est la toile de Pénélope,"* is a figure of speech that refers to an endless obligation, or chore."

[*See also:* Iphigenia at Aulis]

TOPOCATEPELT

This is either an Aloïsianism or a misspelling of Popocatépetl, a neovolcanic mountain range in Mexico.

[*See also:* Cordilliaries]

24 VOLCANOES

1. The North American "Cascade Range" contains 24 volcanoes.
2. The Andes range also contains 24 volcanoes.

VALLATON PAUL BRIDEL AND SAILLENS

JPF in *Mappemonde* links these characters to a theology professor and a pastor in Lausanne.

[*See also:* Chamorel; Heim]

THE BURNING OF BALTHASAR

1. Balthazar was one of the three Magi kings. 2. Baldassare Castiglione, the Renaissance author who died of a high fever, was immortalized in a portrait by Raphael and was a confidant of the de Medicis. 3. Or there is Gérard Balthasar, who shot and killed William the Silent in 1548 and is considered to be the first political assassin to successfully use a handgun. His capture, torture, and eventual execution are detailed in Michel Foucault's *Discipline and Punish:* "The magistrates decreed that the right hand of Gérard

should be burned off with a red-hot iron, that his flesh should be torn from his bones with pincers in six different places..."

[*See also:* Marie Stuart; Transfiguration of Raphael]

PASTOR HENNINKE
Chaplain of Kaiser Wilhelm II; Aloïse worked for Henninke as a governess.

[*See also:* Guillaume II]

DRYANDER
Ernst Dryander, as Aloïse explains, was a chaplain for Kaiser Wilhelm II and also "Castle Preacher" of the Trinity Church in Berlin. He accompanied Wilhelm on international voyages and seems to have been closer to the imperial family than Henninke.

[*See also:* Guillaume II]

CAMILLE DELESSERT
Postal Director for Lausanne, Switzerland.

LÉON XIII
Born Gioacchino Vincenzo Raffaele Luigi, Pope Leon XII was elected pope in 1878, and died in 1903.

ÉCRIT SUR UNE FEUILLE DE PAPIER D'ARGENT / WRITING ON SILVER PAPER
between 1924-1942

PREGNY
Pregny-Chambésy is a commune in the canton of Geneva in Switzerland.

PIE X
"Pio," or "Pius," is the Catholic pope who beatified Joan of Arc. He also banned women from singing in Catholic Church choirs in 1903. In his text *Ad Diem Illium,* written for the 50th Anniversary

of the dogma of the Immaculate Conception, Pius X states that the virtues of the true Mariology should "excite a singular fervor in the souls of Christians," and that it is the key to the "restoration of all things in Christ." The Pope, who was already in poor health at the outbreak of the First World War, was apparently sent into a state of shock and depression by its atrocities and mounting death toll; this aggravated his fragile state and is said to have lead to his early death. The pope's canonization was not until 1954.

PADEREWSKY

Ignace Jan Paderewsky was a composer, pianist, orator, statesman, humanitarian activist, and Prime Minister of Poland following the First World War.

RUMINE

Gabriel Rumine, descendent of Russian aristocracy, was born in Lausanne, Switzerland in 1841. He died in 1871, having bequeathed to the city 1.5 million francs with which to construct the Palais Rumine, a public edifice. The Palace was inaugurated in 1906. The building, sited on Lausanne's Place de la Riponne, originally housed the University of Lausanne; its proximity to City Hall made it appealing as a public space.

[*See also:* Ismet Pacha; White of Riponne]

COPPET

Coppet is a small canton in Pays de Vaud, Switzerland. A castle of this name, in the canton of Coppet, dating back to the 13th century, changed families several times. It received notoriety from its 18th century inhabitant, Jacques Necker, Louis XVI's finance minister, but the castle is best known as the stomping grounds of "The Coppet Group." Necker's daughter, Mme. Germaine de Staël (Anne-Louise Germaine Necker, baroness of Staël Holstein) gathered at Coppet a cadre of literary elite, including Talleyrand, Montmorency, and Jaucourt. The Coppet Group was highly

controversial in Napoleon's France for its inclusion of French
exiles and the provocative writings of its members.

[*See also:* Bernardin de St. Pierre; Chateau de Montaulieu (of
Beaulieu); Kervadec; Le Sacre de Napoléon; Monsieur de Coppet;
Rosalie of the Chablière; The Intuition of Byron]

BRODEQUIN OF THALIE

The phrase *"des brodequins à Thalie"* refers to the boots worn by
Thalia the Greek goddess. Associated with playfulness and joyful-
ness, Thalia is the muse of comedy. The phrase suggests both
the shoes themselves and the mythic being of their wearer. "Les
brodequins," was also a sort of Medieval torture.

À MADEMOISELLE ROSINE / TO MADEMOISELLE ROSINE
nd > 1942

ALBERT MÉRAT

Mérat was a late 19th century French poet. He was very close
friends with Paul Verlaine and Arthur Rimbaud, and is considered part of the Parnassian literary movement, which revived the
sonnet as a popular form. Reacting against the romantic and flowery poetry of the time, this movement focused on the formalities
of crafting prose. His poem "À Mademoiselle Rosine," as published in *Chansons et Madrigaux* (1902):

> *Vous êtes grande en tout comme les blés en mai,*
> *Et votre main n'est pas plus large qu'une rose.*
> *Pour votre pied, ma chère enfant, c'est autre chose*
> *Le prince qu'épousa Cendrillon l'eut aimé.*
> *Comme artiste, le geste est bon, le ton formé.*
> *Et vous chantez, comment dirai-je? ... en virtuose;*
> *Et vous avez déjà, bien avant d'être éclose,*
> *Un petit goût à vous, piquant et parfumé.*
> *Je sais que vous avez dix ans, Mademoiselle,*
> *Et que vous êtes grande, et qu'il faut qu'on cisèle*
> *Ses vers. Si vous alliez ne pas les trouver bons!*

Vous êtes, mon bébé, quasiment une femme.
Acceptez mon hommage et recevez. Madame,
Sans rougir du présent, ce cornet de bonbons.

VICTORIA HALL
Geneva's Victoria Hall was built in the late 19th century and named for Queen Victoria. It is known for its sumptuously decorated interior, with gold-leafed ceiling stucco and a crimson-red color scheme.

PRIÈRE POUR LA BRETAGNE ... L'ÉPOUSE DU BARDE
"Prayer for Brittany" and "The Wife of the Bard," are two poems by Jean-Pierre Calloc'h that appear in his 1921 edition of *À Genoux* (*On my Knees*).

JEAN-PIERRE CALLOC'H
Jean-Pierre-Hyacinthe Calloc'h, or Yann-Ber Kalloc'h in his native language Breton (a French dialect), is best known for his poetry written in Breton. *"Me 'zo Ganet kreiz ar e mor"* or "I was born at sea" is perhaps his best known poem and appears in the same collection as "Prière pour la Bretagne" and "L'épouse du Barde." Calloc'h died defending France during the First World War.

[*See also:* Mistral and Mirielle; Pardon of Ploërmel; Pierre]

PRESIDENT LEBRUN
Before being elected president of France's Third Republic (1932–1940) Albert François Lebrun served in several other political positions. Of note here is his role as Minister of the Government of Colonies in Caillaux.

LECORRE AT MONTBENON IN LAUSANNE
Most likely this is J. Lecorre, an orchestra conductor in Lausanne, noted in a history of orchestral performances in the region. Montbenon is a grand esplanade in the commune of Lausanne, on which are situated the Chapel of Guillaume Tell, the Palace of Justice, and marble statues.

Christomanos

Constantine Christomanos "spoke Greek" to Empress Elizabeth of Hapsburg, as one of the Greek lecturers she employed to read to her whilst strolling the gardens. He later became an accomplished playwright, poet, and journalist, causing a sensation by describing his romantic feelings for the Empress.

[*See also:* l'Achilleion; Hôtel de Caux]

Château de Montaulieu (of Beaulieu)

"Montaulieu" is probably Baroness Isabelle de Montolieu, late 18th century Vaudoise writer and translator, author of *Les Châteaux Suisses, Anciennes Anecdotes et Chroniques* [*Swiss Châteaus: Tales and Anecdotes*]. In her fictive portrait of Jean Jacques Rousseau, entitled *Le Serin de Jean-Jacques Rousseau*, a young girl named Rosine befriends an aged, paranoid, and hermitic Rousseau. Several of the authors whose works she translated were close friends of Madame de Staël; if Montolieu and de Staël were not close friends, they certainly must have been acquainted. The Château de Beaulieu was once Madame de Staël's residence (before Coppet) and is now the home of the *Collection d'Art Brut*.

[*See also:* Coppet; Monsieur de Coppet]

Rosalie of the Chablière

Rosalie de Constant, cousin of Benjamin Constant, acquaintance of Madame de Staël, was a friend of other Vaud writers and artists including Madame Montolieu. Rosalie's *chef d'œuvre* is the painted herbarium she constructed over the course of 40 years. La Chablière was the de Constant family residence in Lausanne.

[*See also:* Coppet]

Bernardin de Saint Pierre

Saint Pierre was an 18th century French writer and botanist. His most famous work, *Paul et Virginie*, was shared by the literary circle of Suzanne Necker (Madame de Staël's mother). The *Bernardin de Saint Pierre* was the name given to a shipping-steamer, which voyaged in the years between World Wars.

[*See also:* Coppet; Monsieur de Coppet; Pierre]

FOLDA DE PIE XII

The Fulda Conference is a meeting of German bishops. The 1931 Conference decided the position of the Catholic Church on Hitler's agenda. Pious XII was widely criticized for not distancing the Church more from Nazi Germany. A *New York Times* article from December 25, 1942 praises the Pope's Christmas Day speech, in which he states: "He who would have the star of peace shine out and stand guard over society should cooperate for his part in giving back to the human person the dignity given to it by God from the beginning; he should oppose the excessive herding of men; as if they were a mass without a soul...."

WALESWSKA AT FINKENSTEIN

The Countess Marie Walewska of Poland was Napoleon Bonaparte's mistress from 1806 until his exile to Saint Helena. In the Countess' memoirs, she records that she gave herself to the emperor as a sacrifice for her country's independence—bartering herself for Poland's sovereignty. When Napoleon moved his military headquarters to the Finkenstein Palace in East Prussia, the Countess accompanied him. Although she gave birth to a child, their son was never publicly recognized as legitimate. International society circles referred to her as Napoleon's "Polish Wife" until they had both divorced their first spouses and remarried other members of the aristocracy.

[*See also:* Napoleon Bonaparte]

JC LAVATER

Johann Kaspar Lavater was an 18th century Swiss poet and physiognomist. Lavater wrote in German, but much of his work circulated throughout France and England. He was a close friend of Goethe's and is better remembered for his poetry than for his writings on physiognomy.

[*See also:* La Lauterbrunn; Werther]

DENISE DUPRAZ
Swiss late 19th and early 20th century poet.

MAURICE PALÉOLOGUE
Paléologue was the son of an exiled noble family that resettled in France in the mid 1800s. He is best known for his role as Minister Plenipotentiary to Bulgaria and then to Russia (1901–1917), and for the posthumous publication of his *Journal de l'Affaire Dreyfus* (*Journal of the Dreyfus Affair*). Paléologue is criticized by some and lauded by others for his non-interventionist approach to dealings with the state. Paléologue was also a well-respected writer, nominated to the Académie Française in 1928.

CHÂTEAU SAINT-ANGE
The Château is also called Castel Sant'Angelo and is commonly known as Hadrian's Monument. It was originally constructed in the Second Century A.D. as the mausoleum of emperor Publius Aelius Hadrianus and his descendents. At the end of the plague of 590 A.D. Saint Michael the Archangel appeared atop the monument sheathing his sword. The building is officially named for this legendary miracle, which is also memorialized in a bronze sculpture by Flemish sculptor Peter Anton von Verschaffelt situated atop the structure. The château served, for a time, as the local prison, and appears as such in several literary works, including Puccini's *Tosca*.

MONTE MARIO
Monte Mario is the highest hill in Rome and is probably named for Mario Mellini, a cardinal who lived atop it in the 15th century.

[*See also:* Campidoglio; Cérès]

MEYERLING
The 1889 "Mayerling Incident" involved the murder-suicide of the heir apparent to the Emperor of Austria, Crown Prince Rudolf of Austria, and his mistress, the Baroness Mary Vetsera. Though married to the Princess Stéphanie of Belgium, Rudolf privately pursued an affair with the baroness. Their families were apparently aware of this "secret." The Mayerling Incident, which took place at Rudolf's hunting lodge in Lower Austria, has captivated

the imaginations of conspiracy theorists and the Austrian people for over a century. As the murder-suicide conclusion leaves many questions unanswered, various theories suggest that it was a politically motivated double-murder.

FÊTE DES VIGNERONS / WINEGROWER'S FESTIVAL
1944

CÉRÈS

Ceres, also known as Demeter, the goddess of agriculture and fecundity, was seen as the nurturer of mankind. The root of this name is shared with *creator* as well as *cereal*. Her identity is often conflated with that of Tellus (Terra Mater) who embodies the fecund earth itself. The festival of spring, "Cerealia," was traditionally celebrated on April 19. Aventine Hill, the site of her temple, is one of the seven hills of ancient Rome.

[*See also:* Campidoglio; La Terre; Monte Mario]

LA MALIBRAN

Maria Malibran, born in 1808, was the daughter of Manuel del Populo Vicente Garcia. Garcia was employed as music instructor to the daughters of Joachim Murat (Napoleon Bonaparte's brother-in-law and the King of Naples). In 1826, Maria Garcia married Eugène Malibran. She is known as "La Malibran," for the success of her 1828 Paris operatic debut, which was sensationally received by the press and the French elite. She died at the age of 28 after having being thrown from a horse.

[*See also:* Cimarosa Cime; Le Sacre]

LHENGRIN

Richard Wagner's *Lohengrin* was originally produced in 1850 in Weimar Germany, under the direction of Franz Liszt. Wagner was not to hear the finished production of this masterpiece for 14 years after its completion—11 years after its debut—as he spent those years exiled from Germany.

QUADRILLE 4 HANDS SACHA GUITRY

The 1938 film *Quadrille,* written, directed, and starring Sacha Guitry is the story of a bizarre love-square, or rather, the story of two couples with intertwining love interests. Guitry was a much-celebrated early 20th century actor, director, and writer who distinguished himself within the cinema milieu for his theatricality. Though criticized for acting on film as one would act for the stage, his exaggerated speech and movement would have appealed to Aloïse.

NÉRON

This opera by Anton Rubenstein, first performed in 1894, is loosely based on the life of the Roman Emperor Nero. "Néron" might also reference the emperor himself, but it's more likely that the opera, or its main character, is the subject in this passage.

LA LAUTERBRUNN

An area within the Swiss canton of Bern. Goethe found inspiration for his verse in its landscape. The name translates to "many springs" and is generally written in the plural form, "La Lauterbrunnen."

[*See also:* JC Lavater; Werther]

ZAÏRA

Zaïre or *Zara* is a tragic play by Voltaire in which a Christian slave falls in love with her Muslim captor, the sultan. The plot involves missed communications and ends in the murder-suicide of the inter-religious couple. In 1829, Vincenzo Bellini's operatic interpretation of this story was performed for the first time and was terribly received. It was not shown again for 140 years.

[*See also:* Le Grand Horloger; Somnebula]

ESTAVAYER CHÂTEAU

Also called the "Château de Chenaux," the castle is situated in Estavayer-le-Lac in the Vaud Canton of Switzerland.

GOUNOD

Charles Gounod, the French composer, is best remembered for the works *Roméo et Juliette, Faust,* and *Mireille.* Many titles by

Gounod appear in Aloïse's writing, including *Sapho* (libretto by Émile Augier); *The Dove; The Queen of Saba* (libretto by Jules Barbier and Michel Carré); *Philémon et Baucis* (libretto by Barbier and Carré); *Jeanne d'Arc; Heaven has Visited Earth; Marie Stuart,* and *Marguerite.*

[*See also:* Marguerite; Marie Stuart; Mistral and Mireille; Promethean Sphinx; Queen of Saba]

MARIE STUART

Marie Stuart was pronounced Queen of Scotland shortly after her birth, but because of her mother's ties to the French monarchy, she spent most of her early years in France. Having married King Francis II, she became Queen of France as well as Queen of Scotland at the age of 17. Many Roman Catholics add that because she was descended from the Tudor lineage, she was also the Queen of England. King Francis's mother was a descendent of the Medici family.

[*See also:* The Burning of Balthazar; Gounod; Lulu]

POST TENEBRAS LUX

"After Darkness, Light" is a Lutheran and Calvinist motto. It was originally intended to reflect gratitude to God for revealing anew His scriptures within the Protestant faith, minus the encumberments of the Catholic Church.

[*See also:* Transfiguration]

PALACE OUCHY

The Palais d'Ouchy was originally constructed in the early 12th century, though it has undergone several massive reconstructions. Situated along the Lake Léman, the castle is just outside of the city of Lausanne, Switzerland. Since 1885 it has served as a hotel.

LA TRAVIATA ... LADY OF THE CAMILLIAS ... MANON AT SAINT SULPICE

The Story of the Knight Des Grieux and Manon Lescaut was a novel published in the early 1800s by Antoine François Prévost. *Manon* was wildly successful despite the controversy it caused and its nationwide ban. A century after its publication, *Manon* continued to inspire operas and ballets of the same name. *Manon* is also referenced in stage plays, novels, and other operas as a classic romantic drama. Alexandre Dumas' *Lady of the Camellias* is one such example: in an opening scene, the story's protagonist, Marguerite, reveals her obsession with Manon-esque tragedy. Following the success of *Camellias* and its stage adaptation, Giuseppi Verdi set the entire tale to music, calling it *La Traviata*. In Jules Massenet's Manon, Saint Sulpice is the site at which Des Grieux and Manon decide to run away together. Saint Sulpice is also a cathedral in the 6th arrondissement of Paris, and a commune in the Swiss Canton of Vaud.

[*See also:* Denantour de Nesles; Manon LesCaux; Marguerite; Werther]

THE MUTE OF PORTICI
Masaniello, ou la Muette de Portici is an 1828 opera by Daniel-François-Esprit Auber. As the French word for mute, *muette,* can also be translated as "army," the phrase *"la muette des halles"* (literally, the army of the halls), refers to the character of a notoriously bossy, insolent, or foul-mouthed woman.

[*See also:* Manon LesCaux]

MANON LESCAUX
Daniel-François-Esprit Auber's operatic interpretation of *Manon,* or the original novel by Prévost.

[*See also:* La Traviata...; The Mute of Portici]

HÔTEL DE CAUX
Formerly the Grand Hôtel de Caux, the Hotel Regina in Montreux Switzerland supposedly inspired the castle in Disney's *Snow White*. The Hotel's history includes some intriguing tales. In 1898, Elizabeth "Sissa" Hapsbourg, the Empress of Austria, suffered an assassination attempt while vacationing in the hotel. In 1944, the Hôtel provided refuge to over 1500 Hungarian Jews rerouted from their Auschwitz destination.

SOMNEBULA
La Sonnambula is an 1831 opera by Vicenzo Bellini. The title translates to "The Sleepwalker."

[*See also:* Zaïre]

PIERRE CHANLAINE
Born Pierre Wunstel, Chanlaine was a writer, journalist, and president of the association of *"Écrivains Combattants,"* a literary association for veterans of war. Aloïse mentions the following of his titles in her writings: *Mam'zelle Bonaparte, The Short and Painful Life of the King of Rome,* and *Clarisse is Tenacious.*

[*See also:* Clarisse Harlowes; Pierre]

CLARISSE HARLOWES
Clarissa remains one of the longest novels written in the English language. Completed in 1748, Samuel Richardson's tale follows the life of the young, beautiful, and courageous Clarissa Harlowe. That her name is made plural in this text suggests the ubiquity of the prototypically perfect young woman in literature.

CARNIVAL OF VENICE
"Carnival of Venice" is a folk song. It is also the name of the annual carnival in Venice.

ARCHANGEL OF GAMBETTA
Léon Gambetta served as French premier for ten years following the fall of Napoleon's Second Empire (1881–82) and assisted in the rebuilding of France during the provisional government years. "Archangel Gambetta" is perhaps derived from Archangel Gabriel.

MÉNÉLIK
Probably Sahle Maryam, or Emperor Ménélik II of Ethiopia, who ruled from 1889–1913.

ISMET PACHA
Later called, "İsmet İnönü," Pacha served as Prime Minister of Turkey from 1923–1937 and from 1961–1965, and served as the country's second president from 1938–1950. Pacha was also

present for the July 24, 1923 Signing of the Treaty of Lausanne. This peace treaty, which repartitioned the Ottoman Empire and recognized sovereignty of the Turkish state, was signed at the Palais Rumine. *"Une vie de pacha"* (literally, a life of pasha) is a figure of speech implying supreme comfort, luxuriousness, and ease.

[*See also:* Holy War of 1912; Rumine; White of the Riponne]

TSARTORISKY
Possibly Prince Tsartoriski, the interim Chancellor of the Russian Empire, who replaced Count Woronzow in 1804.

DENANTOUR DE NESLES
A Swiss travel guide from 1822 refers to Denantour as a beautiful country home in Lausanne, situated in a magnificent position. The Tour de Nesles itself was a guard tower constructed along the Seine in Paris during the 13th century. A 15th century scandal, involving Marguerite de Bourgogne later became the subject of Alexander Dumas's *Le Tour de Nesles*.

[*See also:* La Traviata...; Marguerite]

THE ARTIST KNIE
Possibly "Oscar Knie," a character in Jacques Copeau's *Comédie Nouvelle*. More likely, this refers to the Family Knie, known as the "Cirque Variété National Suisse Frères Knie," which began in the 1850s and continues today in its fourth generation.

KERVADEC
This is actually *Capitaine Kernadec,* the comedy by Madame de Staël, written in 1810 over the course of several days for the purpose of lightening the mood of the troubled Napoleonic era. Liliane de Kermadec, the French director and writer, produced the biographic-fiction *Aloïse* in 1975, which was loosely based on the life of Aloïse Corbaz. This last reference is only an uncanny coincidence.

[*See also:* Coppet; Delphine Corinne]

Genevieve of Candia

François de Candie was the first viscount of Geneva in the early 14th century. Descendant of the noble House of Candia, he began his career in military service, eventually being accepted into the Most Noble Order of the Priory of Geneva. He turned the position of viscount into one of ambassadorial importance through the international dialogue he generated with the greater European powers.

Pardon of Ploërmel

Also called "Dinorah," the *Pardon of Ploërmel* is a 19th century comic opera by Giacomo Meyerbeer. The work was most acclaimed for the protagonist's *coloratura* solos, which are said to evince her imbalanced mental state and her levity of being. The words are based on a folktale from Brittany involving the custom of annual pilgrimage to the local shrine of the Virgin.

[*See also:* Jean-Pierre Calloc'h; Jenny Lind]

The Intuition of Byron

Né George Gordon Byron, the 6th Baron Byron is commonly known as Lord Byron. A friend of Germaine de Staël, Byron spent the latter part of his life in self-imposed exile in Geneva. His exile from England was most likely spurred by his embarrassment over allegations of incest, sodomy, and other sexual misdeeds. While in Switzerland he also befriended Mary Shelley and her husband Percy Bysshe Shelley.

[*See also:* Coppet; Walter Scott]

Queen Zita

The Empress Zita of Austria was born the Princess of Bourbon-Parma in the last decade of the 19th century. She and her husband, Charles of Austria, ascended to the throne following the assassination of Franz Ferdinand and his wife Sophie. Exiled from Austria after the First World War, Zita, Charles and their eight children initially settled in Switzerland. After Charles' early demise in 1922, the family moved around Spain, Belgium, the United States, and Luxembourg, finally resettling in Austria in the 1980s. Zita's beatification is currently being petitioned.

PIERREFONTAINE
Pierre François Léonard Fontaine worked in life-long collaboration with Charles Percier. Named Imperial Architects of Napoleon's court in 1801, Fontaine and Percier designed much of Paris's iconic grandeur. The two were responsible for the planning and design of the Tuileries Palace and the Arc de Triomphe, as well as reconstructions of the Château Fontainbleau, the Louvre, the Château of Versailles, and many other sites.

[*See also:* Pierre; Sans-Souci]

FRANCIS CARCO
Carco was a French poet and novelist and one of the founders of *L'école fantaisiste*, the "fantasy school." His friends included Picasso, Apollinaire, Max Jacob, and Modigliani. A frequenter of the then-seedy Montmartre neighborhood of Paris, many of his writings experiment with *argot* (slang) and describe the rougher edges of French society.

MISTRAL AND MIREILLE
The French poet Frédéric Mistral was awarded the Nobel Prize in 1904. His best-known epic poems, of which *Mireille* is one, are written in Provençal French. The composer Gounod later transformed Mireille, published in 1859, into an opera.

[*See also:* Jean-Pierre Calloc'h; Gounod]

WELKERSCHLACHT
This is probably a misspelling of the *Völkerschlacht bei Leipzig,* also known as the Battle of Leipzig or the Battle of Nations. This 1812 battle was the largest of the Napoleonic Wars as well as the largest war in Europe until the First World War. France and her allies were opposed to an allied opposition including Austria, Prussia, Russia and Sweden. The opposition radically outnumbered the French army, which had been decimated by France's unsuccessful invasion of Russia. Napoleon abdicated and shortly thereafter was exiled to the isle of Elba.

[*See also:* Napoleon Bonaparte; Walewska]

The English translation from German is "Victory Avenue." The Siegesalle, originally constructed in 1873, was a main road through Berlin. In 1895, Kaiser Wilhelm II adorned its borders with marble statues of Prussian royalty as a patriotic gift to the German populace. It has since been converted into a footpath, and most of the sculptures have been displaced.

[*See also:* Guillaume II]

THE QUEEN OF SABA

La reine de Saba is an opera by Gounod. She is also a biblical figure.

[*See also:* Gounod]

THE QUEEN ESTHER

Like Saba, Esther was a queen and biblical figure. She is considered among the most important figures recognized during the Jewish holiday Purim.

QUEEN BERTHE

Berthe aux Grands Pieds (or "Bigfoot Bertha") was originally a legend dating back to the 12th century. In this tale, Pepin the Short, King of France, is to marry Berthe the Hungarian princess. The daughter of the king's nursemaid usurps the crown through trickery and sends away the real Berthe. After trials and tribulations, the couple is reunited. Over the centuries, the story has been retold in various formats. In 1878 Victorin Joncières produced an infamous flop in operatic form.

IPHIGENIA AT AULIS

The last known work of Euripides, in which Agamemnon must sacrifice his daughter Iphigenia to the gods so the wind might return and his Greek fleet set sail from Aulis to battle Troy. To convince his wife Clytemnestra to send their daughter to him, Agamemnon writes her a letter stating that he intends to marry Iphigenia to Achilles. The revelation of the truth and its repercussions are not enough to spare Iphigenia's life. Christoph Willibald Gluck's 1774 operatic interpretation is entitled *Iphigénie en Aulide*.

[*See also:* Cythère; L'Achilleion; Pénélope Fabric Terrestrial]

WERTHER

Jules Massenet's opera based on Goethe's *The Sorrows of Young Werther*, premiered in 1892.

[*See also:* JC Lavater; La Lauterbrunn; La Traviata...]

JENNY LIND

Née Johanna Maria Lind, the widely renowned opera singer was dubbed "The Swedish Nightingale." Though she would later count the composers Mendelssohn, Chopin, Meyerbeer, and the writer Hans Christian Andersen among her close friends, Lind was of humble origin and was seen as embodying the modest spirit of the commoner.

[*See also:* Pardon of Ploërmel]

CYTHÈRE

This is most likely in reference to *Cythère assiégée* by Willibald Gluck, the first production of which was an operatic comedy, the second an opera-ballet.

[*See also:* Iphigenia at Aulis]

DELFINE CORINNE

Delfine and *Corinne* are works by Germaine de Staël.

[*See also:* Coppet; Kervadec; Monsieur de Coppet]

SAINT LÉGIER

Saint Légier-La Chiésaz is a Swiss commune in the canton of Vaud, close to Montreux and Vevey.

[*See also:* Chiesa of Saint Pére Bênoit]

LA COUPE DE THULÉ
La coupe du roi de Thulé is a Georges Bizet opera from 1869.

BAZAR BÉCHERT
Louis Béchert was Vaud tea importer based in Lausanne in the early 20th century.

BÉATRICE D'ESTE
1. This refers to the composition by French composer Reynaldo Hahn entitled *Le Bal de Béatrice d'Este,* from 1909. 2. Or it refers to the portrait of Béatrice by Leonardo da Vinci, circa 1490. 3. Or else it refers directly to Béatrice d'Este, who was duchess of Milan during the Renaissance and is credited with much influence over the arts and fashion of the time. From a 1907 biographical account of her personal life, one can ascertain that she lived something of a romantic tragedy.

THE MIKADO
The Mikado is the title of a satiric comic-opera by Gilbert and Sullivan from 1885.

[*See also:* Tepsis]

CIMAROSA CIME
1. "Cima Rosa" translates to "Rose Mount." The Monte Rosa is the second largest mountain in the Alps and is part of the Pennine Alps, which are shared by Italy and Switzerland. 2. The composer and organist Dominico Cimarosa is best remembered for his sacred compositions, and for the multitude of operatic works he produced (76 in all). Cimarosa was also the *maestro di cappella* in Catherine's St. Petersburg cathedral, *Kapellmeister* of Emperor Leopold II cathedral in Vienna, and the first organist of the royal church in Naples.

[*See also:* La Malibran]

THE VIOLET OF SCHILLER
"The Violet" is a poem by Friedrich von Schiller, originally written in German.

BILLET À L'INCONNUE / TICKET TO THE UNKNOWN
23 May 1947

MADONNA OF CORSICA

Most likely this refers to the Madonna statue at Col del Bavella to which thousands of pilgrims still flock every year, in the hope of witnessing miracles.

TEPSIS

As an alternative spelling of Thepsis, *Tepsis* is the Greek father of drama. Gilbert & Sullivan's first collaboration, entitled *Thepsis* or *The Gods Grown Old,* was a spectacular success in 1870s England. This opera follows a troupe of comedic actors on their quest to replace aging and ineffective gods. The gods find their replacements unsuitable and their ineffective rule embarrassing, and banish them back to the earth to be "eminent tragedians, whom no one ever goes to see."

[*See also:* The Mikado]

WHITE OF THE RIPONNE

This probably refers to the white marble of Place de la Riponne in Lausanne, the site of the Palais Rumine.

[*See also:* Ismet Pacha; Rumine]

DE GAULE

1. De Gaule refers either to the Gauls or to Charles de Gaulle, the French president (1959–1969). While it is true that Charles de Gaulle was only later celebrated, Aloïse *may* have known of his heroism in the First World War. 2. Or, and perhaps this is most likely, she refers here to Dr. Justus Gaule, a Swiss-German professor of physiology.

PROMETHEAN SPHINX

Prometheus is a figure from Greek mythology, the benefactor of humanity who stole fire from the gods to give to man. He is often depicted in paintings in the throes of agony—as punishment for his theft, he was strapped to a rock for all eternity; each day a large eagle would newly devour his liver. In the accounts of Sappho,

Aesop, Ovid, and Plato, Prometheus also bestows upon man the gifts of artistry and civility.

[*See also:* Gounod; Rumine]

HIEROPHANT

In religious ceremony the hierophant leads worshippers to the holy site or the holy figure. It is a messenger between the mortal and immortal realms.

SÉDIA

Sedia gestatoria is the name for the portable throne on which the Pope is carried.

IMPERIAL YERSIN OF BANKNOTE

1. Alexandre Emile Jean Yersin, born in Lausanne, Switzerland in 1863, co-discovered the bacteria that caused the bubonic and pneumonic plagues while studying under the direction of Louis Pasteur in Paris. He did much of his later research in French Indochina, spearheading a team charged with investigating plague epidemics. Eventually settling in Vietnam, Yersin applied his interest in botany to developing the cultivation of rubber trees. 2. JPF offers the most likely association, which is that another Yersin was a doctor at Saint Rosière.

CAMPIDOGLIO OF LYGIE

"Campidoglio" is either the Piazza Campidoglio or the hill on which it is located, one of the Seven Hills of Rome. "Lygie" is Ligia, Greece, a tiny town in Ilia Prefecture. The phrase might refer to a hill just outside of the town of Ligia.

[*See also:* Cérès; Monte Mario]

LIFE OF ALOÏSE CORBAZ

Much of what is written about the fabulous artist is compiled from family stories retold, scant public records, and the artist's own writings and rare revelations. Many uncertainties remain—for example, whether or not she was ever romantically involved with a defrocked priest.

Aloïse Corbaz was born on June 28, 1886 in Lausanne, Switzerland. She took private singing lessons outside of secondary school, and learned to sew very elaborate clothing at the Cantonal Dressmaking school. In school she attained proficiency in English, German, Italian, and Latin, and developed a profound love for and knowledge of opera. Raised Protestant, she voraciously amassed knowledge of Biblical verse and was active in her local church.

Her 'lost love,' Joseph Sauvage, a defrocked Catholic priest, was a Protestant theology student living with her brother close by. Their romance seems to have been quite short and mostly communicated in amorous and flowery letters. Aloïse's older sister, Marguerite, intervened in the affair—out of malice, jealousy, or concern, it's not clear—and ended the budding relationship. As Aloïse's aspirations to become a famous singer faded, and perhaps fleeing from the scene of her broken heart, she was sent to work as a private governess in Germany.

Not much is known about Aloïse's time as governess, but at age 25 she worked in Pottsdam as a private instructor and *au pair* for the children of the chaplain of Kaiser Wilhelm II. Though the two probably never met, Aloïse fell in love with the emperor. Perhaps this was her ideal situation: tending children not her own, living in close proximity to a man she loved but could not have; this, intermingled with the "entire Gotha of European aristocracy." Her girlhood fantasies, inspired by her love of opera with its decadence and tragic romance, became her immediate reality.

Just before the outset of the first World War, Aloïse was sent back to Lausanne where she became an active pacifist. In early 1918 she was admitted to the psychiatric hospital at Cery. After two years in which her condition continued to degrade, her doctors decided she was incurable. During this time, Aloïse created her first drawings and writings—her most lucid writings, those most clearly relating to the real world, were written there—and piqued the interests of Drs. Saussure and Steck. In late 1920 she was transferred to the Rosière Home in Gimel (a hospital for the chronically ill), where she sank into what Porret-Forel referred to as something of an autistic state. Until 1933 she allowed herself to follow compulsions towards "anger, jealousy, lustful displays and outbursts." Thereafter she began developing a "parallel autistic exploration," involving the collection of scraps of papers for drawing and obsessive ironing in the hospital laundry room. The drawings served as an outlet for her other-worldly explorations, while ironing was a form of practical participation in the physical reality of the asylum.

Her doctor, biographer, and interpreter Jacqueline Porret-Forel writes of Aloïse, "when she was admitted to the Cery Psychiatric Hospital on February 21, 1918, she entered her own existential death. Later, her intense vitality would allow her to exist once again, but this could only take place as it were, within another trans-substantial species, in the Eucharistic sense of the word." In 1963, the Cantonal Fine Arts Museum in the Palais de Rumine in Lausanne invited Aloïse to exhibit

her drawings in conjunction with an exhibit of Swiss women paint-
ers. The exhibition was successful in drawing public attention to her
work, but it was disastrous for the artist's psyche, and she died several
months later.

AGAINST INTERPRETATION

"All of Aloïse's pictoral œuvre proceeds from her cosmological conception, formed from her schizophrenic condition, which ... flourished into a triumphant and autonomous creation. It is therefore necessary to define the principles of this cosmology to understand the implications of each of her drawings: the ancient world of other-times (le monde ancien d'autrefois) no longer exists, and Aloïse becomes the royal earth thrown into space; then the Creator who reigns over all of the universe that comes forth from her paintbrush; the Solar Ricochet (*Ricochet Solaire*) fertilizes this earth and causes, with its caress, the unlimited multitude of images whose power she captures; the Trinity in Alternative Consubstantiality (*Trinité en Consubstantialité Alternative*) restores unity to her dissociated person; it also allows the free, universal, and simultaneous passage of forms and myriad substances that compose her fractured ego. The polyvalence of forms and personages begins from there."[1]

* * *

All of Jacqueline Porret-Forel's expository texts revealing the cosmology of Aloïse Corbaz are formed of the objectivity and scientific methodology with which she approached her subject. Porret-Forel was cautious of imposing her own subjective interpretations; her self-distancing from Aloïse compelled her to seek out the intrinsic logic buried within the text. An imposed interpretation could have flourished into a triumphant and autonomous creation, if not for the respect and regard she maintained for Aloïse. As Jacqueline Porret-Forel was Aloïse Corbaz's friend and primary biographer, examining her role and reading her texts alongside those of Aloïse is essential to a consideration of Aloïse and her work. She allowed for the free, universal, and simultaneous clarifying of forms and myriad associations that compose Aloïse's fractured ego to reveal themselves to her.

PRIMARY AUTOBIOGRAPHERS

Jacqueline Porret-Forel first learned of Aloïse's drawings in the context of her doctoral studies in medicine. Being a doctor, she was interested in the mind behind the drawings, and her dissertation evinced her effort to understand Aloïse's life and works as one. As her relationship with Aloïse and her works deepened, Jacqueline went on to explain her understanding of the artist's cosmology and to decrypt Aloïse's texts and drawings in even greater depth. When Jacqueline encountered "Art Brut," a concept advanced by French artist Jean Dubuffet incorporating what had formerly been called "psychiatric art," she augmented her analytic methodology with that of art criticism and reconsidered Aloïsian aesthetics in the context of art history. Her role as Aloïse's personal liaison to the *ancient world of other times* (the real world outside the asylum) and her ongoing role as decryptor and translator were thus formed in tandem. Unlike Dubuffet and many other artist-writers, Jacqueline possessed neither self-serving motives (such as that of

---

[1]   Jacqueline Porret-Forel, *Aloïse* (Art Brut Compagnie, Paris 1948), 104. My translation.

furthering an aesthetic movement), nor cumbersome prejudices about what "Art" ought to be.

A primary biographer—which Jacqueline became for Aloïse—almost always plays an integral role in the "discovery" and promotion of artists termed "Art Brut" or "Outsider,"[2] because creators working on the margins of culture often have no interest in or lack the means to publicize their works and lives. Either by externally-imposed exile or by way of self-segregation, the Art Brut or Outsider artist is very much isolated from cultural resources. Outsider Artists are generally social outcasts; they are found among the homeless, the clinically or unclinically insane, religious zealots, and obsessive tinkerers and constructors of all stripes. Unifying characteristics include their overwhelming drive toward creation—defying an absence of artistic training—and some degree of social alienation or ostracization. For their works to receive exposure, these artists require some sort of intervention in the form of translator or personal ambassador to the world at large. Of course, many marginalized artists do not welcome "discovery" and their works are not created in anticipation of publicity. The works of Outsider and Art Brut artists are largely inspired by personal experience and therefore exist as highly subjective narratives. As super-subjective creators, the intended audience most often remains undefined or unconsidered, or, the artists create for themselves alone. The works of Outsider and Art Brut artists are largely inspired by personal experience. And, unlike the fine artist, the Outsider is either ignorant of or removed from the larger narrative of Art History and cultural trends.

Though the pairing of Outsider artist and biographer is an essential one, the terms and depth of the relationships vary. If the exposure does not drastically alter the work or psychologically damage the creator; if the artist-biographer relationship is founded on trust, amicability, and shared enthusiasm for the artworks; if the artist and historian find some measure of mutual fulfillment through this bond; then perhaps it can then be said that their relationship was fruitful. And perhaps the greatest success is one in which the artist's and historian's

---

2   "Outsider Art" or "Self-Taught Art" or "Folk Art," as it is called in the United States and Britain, shares many of the artists and characteristics of Art Brut. Art Brut is however a more conceptually specific phenomenon, which I will address in greater detail further on.

names become inextricably bound—Charles Shannon + Bill Traylor, Walter Morgenthaler + Adolph Wölfli, Tarmo Pasto + Martin Ramirez, Jacqueline Porret-Forel + Aloïse Corbaz—such that one must read the artwork through the primary biographer's analysis (as well as on its own). Texts written about an artist by his or her primary biographer offer insight into the artist's life history and into the impetus to create, document, and historicize the work.

Perhaps my description of the artist-biographer relationship expresses a willful optimism. But in each of the collaborative examples cited, the shared enthusiasm for the artworks also fostered a mutual enthusiasm for the interpersonal relationship. In those examples, the cultural ambassador furnished the artist with materials, communicated with him or her regularly, in some cases assisted with room and board, and generally became one of the closest persons to the artist's alternate reality (and so the most familiar to and welcome in their universe). It bears reiteration that marginalized artists are at least initially indifferent or opposed to sharing their private universe. After all, they'd created their own niche existences, having found themselves ill-fitted (or been found ill-fitted) to the greater whole of society.

Put otherwise, artists create to express that which is ineffable, to represent that which exceeds the bounds of their articulable language. If, in addition, these artists create for themselves alone—without consideration of effective external communication—the richness of the resulting oeuvre might remain forever entombed within its own self-reflexive complexity. The self-specific language is so unique and so alien that it either goes unheard (is inaudible within the din of cultural phenomena) or is dismissed as incomprehensible (and thus invalid within the contemporary cultural narrative). *I draw what I see ... I write when I can't see what it is ...* said Aloïse, and the words and images envisioned were made real when penned to paper. A gesture so pure, and in the service of such an unimaginably grand undertaking, might have vanished into the realm of unwritten histories, eternally encrypted manuscripts, and discarded chefs d'oeuvre, without the intervention of an interlocutor, an interpreter.

As any artist's portrait is a self-portrait, so the historian's portrait of an artist bears the historian's likeness. Examining the traces of subjectivity left by art historians within the biographies they write yields a portrait of the biographer as well. In studying the work of Outsider and Art Brut artists, whose biographies inevitably enter into discussion of their oeuvre, one must keep in mind both portraits. This is particularly important for the secondary historian, a viewer excluded from direct interaction with the artist. The super-subjectivity of Aloïse's drawings and writings necessitates an understanding of the artist—her history, preferences, manner of speaking and moving, and so on. Thus, much of Porret-Forel's exploration of Aloïse's drawings is contingent on her understanding of Aloïse Corbaz, and much of reading Aloïse now is contingent on understanding their two bodies of work in tandem. Our picture of her oeuvre is a product of Porret-Forel's original impression and is imprinted with her image.

JACQUELINE PORRET FOREL & HANS STECK

Contemporary research on and exhibitions of Aloïse Corbaz's work find their origins in the unflagging fascination and investigations of Dr. Jacqueline Porret-Forel and her professor Dr. Hans Steck. Dr Steck, director of the Psychiatric Hospital in Cery, Switzerland from 1936-1960, was keenly interested in the advantages of incorporating medical teaching and artistic creation into the psychiatric hospital setting. Under his direction, the terms aliéné (insane, alienated) and asile (asylum) were dropped from the institutional rhetoric, reflecting a re-visioning of mental illness as treatable and the hospital as a site of restorative services rather than a cloister for the socially misfitted. Steck and his contemporaries, doctors Hans Prinzhorn, Alfred Bader, and Walter Morgenthaler—directors of similarly revolutionary psychiatric hospitals in Europe—collected and documented their patients' artistic creations and catalyzed a movement to consider the work of mental patients as fine art. Hans Steck's collection of "gribouillages" is particularly notable: he considered these productions a testament to his patients' overall wellbeing, presenting an inroad to a better understanding of their condition.

Steck's methodological cataloging of his patients' creations is evidence of the seriousness and compassion with which he approached his task. He recorded the individual's ideal atmosphere and preferred method of working, the frequency of artistic activity, the type of materials used, and the overall progression of the work. He considered these products aesthetically and conceptually, not just as medical specimens or evidence of the particularities of illness. In her essay "Hans Steck ou le Parti Pris de la Folie," Lucienne Peiry, directrice of the Art Brut Collection in Lausanne, writes:

> *Hans Steck envisaged this creation as a form of reaction against the illness, a manner of creating anew one's position of superiority, [and] of domination over the destructive tendencies of mental illness ... [the ill] liberate themselves by this game of creative imagining....*[3]

Steck lived in Zurich at the height of the Dadaist movement and was in conversation with its founders, many of whom were influenced by Prinzhorn's 1922 publication of *Bildnerei der Geisteskranken* (Artistry of the Mentally Ill). These artists decried rationality, the academy, and staid culture. Steck's understanding of the agenda fueling the Dadaist and Surrealist movements, as well as their antagonistic and then-revolutionary aesthetics, was useful in later conceiving of his patients' creations as art.

Steck's relationship with the interned, their work, his students, and the hospital is perhaps best illustrated in a photograph taken during his last clinical seminar on "The Patient's Artistic Creation." His students, seated in the foreground, attentively observe what appears to be a conversation between Aloïse Corbaz and Dr. Steck. Aloïse, her hair neatly done up and wearing a cardigan, faces away from the camera and away from the students, addressing the doctor, who leans forward into her words. Twelve of her small portraits and a large scroll drawing hang salon-style on the wall behind, serving as a backdrop for this scene. It's a very theatrical set-up—students as audience, drawings as backdrop, and Aloïse and the doctor as protagonists—but oddly so. The scene's significance lies in the placement of the artist and the inquiry before the work, and in the discussion of both. She faces her work—it is her audience. He faces his students—they are his audience. Neither is presenting the work. Neither is addressing either audience. Rather the

---

3   Lucienne Peiry, *La mentalité et la pensée magique chez les schizophrènes* (Primitive Mentality and Magical Thinking among Schizophrenics), in Alfred Bader's *Petit Maîtres de la Folie* (Lausanne: La Guide du livre et Éditions Clairefontaine, 1961), 9–10.

focus is the conversation between doctor and patient, observing and observed by their respective universes.

The only surviving drawings of Aloïse's early period are those fastidiously collected by Dr. Steck. His keen interest in the patient, her oeuvre, and her psychic development led him to introduce her to his student Jacqueline Porret-Forel, who had first seen Aloïse's drawings in Steck's classroom in 1939. Two years later, recollecting the images she'd seen in Dr. Steck's seminar, Porret-Forel decided to seek out their creator. Having gone on assignment to Gimel Hospital to provide routine care for a patient with pneumonia,[4] she sought out Aloïse, who was also interned there. In Muriel Edelstein's documentary *Sans Souci, l'art d'Aloïse*, Dr. Forel says, "At first, I didn't like Aloïse as Aloïse, but because she was the creator of those drawings."[5] Their first encounters, during which Aloïse famously hissed at her "Allez-vous en! Vous n'avez pas de couleur!", were less than amicable, but in subsequent visits Aloïse began to reveal herself and the particularities of her universe. Porret-Forel furnished the artist with drawing materials, brought little cadeaux, "chatted"[6] with Aloïse, and provided the emotional support of friendship. Aloïse eventually baptized her with the monikers Ange Forel and Doctoresse Carola. And Jacqueline reminisces fondly, "If I were a vegetable, Aloïse would be the earth ... she breathed a sort of life into me."[7] Jacqueline and Aloïse's friendship lasted till the end of Aloïse's life in 1964 and inspired what has become Porret-Forel's life-long project.

Jacqueline Porret-Forel's texts are singular documents, which afford a unique proximity to the artist. Her early writing is analytical but respectful of her relationship with the artist; it reads nothing like an aesthetic critique. Her doctoral thesis, entitled *Aloyse: ou la Peinture*

---

4   During World War II, medical practitioners were deployed to various Swiss hospitals to fill in for those doctors assisting with the war-effort.

5   Muriel Edelstein, *Sans Souci, l'Art d'Aloïse* (Paris, Long Par Court, Absynthe Productions 2000) 54'.

6   Although most words were entirely incomprehensible to the listener.

7   Ibid.

Magique d'une Schizophrène[8] and published in 1953, discusses a "pathological art and its symbolic realization which seem analogous to that
of primitive art having a magical origin and motivation."[9] Two things
are immediately apparent in examining *Aloyse*. The first is the misspelling of Aloïse's name; her forename had been previously mis-tran-
scribed from her medical records as "Aloyse," and her surname omitted. The second is constative and only apparent in contrast with Dr.
Porret-Forel's later writings about Aloïse. The terms "pathological" and
"primitive" site the text historically. Primitive is eventually replaced
with terminology more specific to Aloïse's oeuvre, ultimately more
politically correct language. "Pathological art" dates back to a period
in which the creations of mental patients were primarily examined by
doctors for the purpose of decoding the patient's psyche.

Aloyse was written for a doctoral committee in the department of medicine, and not for an art journal or cultural text: this early text most
often refers to Aloïse as la malade or la schizophrène, and discusses
her works in relation to her illness:

> *Aloyse's drawings are also proof that the patient has*
> *not found a normal solution to the problems posed by*
> *femininity. She cannot, due to her illness, due to her*
> *internment ... however she has made an enormous*
> *constructive effort in the course of her illness that has*
> *brought her to the best solution, which has permitted*
> *her psycho-sexual dissociation...*[10]

Although much of *Aloyse* genuinely enters into an aesthetic and con-
ceptual discussion of the artwork, the symbolic/aesthetic analysis is
coupled with an examination of Aloïse-the-patient. For example, in
analyzing a drawing from 1950, Porret-Forel describes the evolution
of love, or a woman's perception thereof, as illustrated by Aloïse. She

---

8   Subsequent analyses of Aloïse's works and life authored by Dr. Porret-Forel are
     Aloïse (Compagnie d'Art Brut, 1948), *Aloïse et son théâtre* (Jaunin, 1953), *Aloïse et le*
     theatre de l'Universe (Skira, 1993), *La voleuse de mappemonde: Les Ecrits d'Aloïse* (Zoë,
     2004), and *Comme un papillon sur elle* (Haretari-Kumottari, 2009) which includes
     English and Japanese translations, and reproductions not previously seen.
9   Porret-Forel, *Aloyse, ou la peinture magique d'une schizophrène* (Lausanne:
     Imprimerie Henri Jaunin, 1953), 8.
10   *Ibid.*, 24.

addresses the symbolic content of the figures' interactions within the drawn landscape: the sphinx illustrated in the piece represents concepts more profound than those immediately apparent to the viewer. Porret-Forel theorizes, "it's a woman who has no body, only a bust, the man is afraid, he doesn't know who this woman is, he is in love with her."[11]

This text was written five years after Jacqueline and Jean Dubuffet met and it is clear that his conceptualization of Art Brut influenced Porret-Forel's analysis of Aloïse in some part. This perhaps partially explains why her thesis departs from standard patient-analysis and also discusses the patient's creations as art.

COMPAGNIE DE L'ART BRUT

When Dubuffet first began his quest for a true naïve art, the blood and guts of the modernist impulse, he'd coined the term "Art Brut," and conceptualized its parameters in advance of actually witnessing it first-hand. His longing for the ineffable rawness that is Art Brut was a metaphor for the movement itself, as the term and its implied referents (art of the insane, social outsiders, mediumnistic creators) predate the formation of an artist roster and a collection of works. Art Brut was not just another case of fetishizing the Outsider (as many have described the relationship between the modernists and ethnographic/Folk-arts). Dubuffet's impulse was a personal response to his own aesthetic sensibility and reflected his disdain for the dominant "academic arts" of the time. The formation of the Art Brut concept and collection was something akin to a spiritual quest, one which ran parallel to Dubuffet's studio practice and his literary works.

In 1945, Jean Dubuffet began amassing artworks for the *Collection de l'Art Brut* (Art Brut Collection). The first exhibition of these findings as a group took place in 1947, at the Galerie René Drouin in Paris. This exhibition was immediately followed by the formation of the *Compagnie de l'Art Brut* (Art Brut Company), an advisory board composed of artists (most notably André Breton), psychiatrists, and writers interested in publicizing the concept by organizing exhibitions,

---

11   *Ibid.*, 24.

discovering new artists, and disseminating their collective discourse in an intermittently published periodical called *Les Fascicules de l'Art Brut*. In 1949, with a large museum exhibition and a manifesto entitled "Art Brut Préféré aux Arts Culturels" (Art Brut Preferred to Cultural Art) to go with it, Dubuffet laid out the Company's agenda. This was to set ablaze the conservative discourse of the cultural elite occupying then-Contemporary Art and to unshackle art produced by the clinically insane from its conscription into "psychiatric" or "pathological" art. Dubuffet's manifesto embodies the spirit of his quest. It is passionately pointed, and at points hilariously heated:

> *True art is never where it is expected to be: in the place where no one considers it, nor names it. Art hates to be recognized and greeted by name; it runs away immediately.... It was in July 1945 that we undertook in both France and Switzerland, then in other countries, methodical research into the relevant ways of producing that which we now call Art Brut.... Our point of view is that art is the same in all cases, and there is no more an art of the mad than there is an art of the dyspeptic, or an art for those with bad knees.*

In 1976, after years of itinerant wandering, the Art Brut Collection finally found a permanent home in Lausanne, Switzerland. Art Brut is not, nor was it ever, a movement per se. Rather, it sprang forth in the form of epiphany, in texts, and in the concept of an "open set" collection—the artists and artworks are representative of an ostensibly infinite whole.

For Dubuffet, Art Brut was intended to jeopardize the stability of the fine art canon. Conceived of as an antagonistic gesture pitted against high culture—enlisting those "marginalized" by this culture—it aimed to contest the meaning and territory of cultural production itself. Dubuffet compared Art Brut to a strange wind blowing up against culture, challenging it to morph and change. But in actuality, Art Brut is neither diametrically opposed to culture, nor marginalized; it is something of a naturally occurring alternative universe ... much in the fashion of those universes created by its artists. One might say it's not

Other, it's another. Michel Thévoz[12] explains in his book *Art Brut* that the success of this group in escaping marginalization and homogenization was that it was able to reveal hidden truths that already existed within mainstream art. Art Brut isn't forced to the margins—in fact, it offers an alternative means of decoding works of "fine art." The decryption techniques necessary for comprehending art created in a highly subjective language provide valuable, alternative methods for rereading contemporary mainstream works.

DUBUFFET & ALOÏSE

Jean Dubuffet and Dr. Jacqueline Porret-Forel first met by chance postal error. In 1947, Jacqueline received a letter from Dubuffet requesting information and drawings for his collection. At this time, while living in Paris, Dubuffet was contacting psychologists and mental hospitals across Europe, collecting works and soliciting artists, writers, and medical professionals for support for the Art Brut Collection. Although the letter was intended for another Dr. Forel living in Switzerland, Porret-Forel seized upon the serendipitous occasion to present Aloïse's drawings to Dubuffet. The unexpected connection introduced both to entirely new worlds—Aloïse would become one of the most important artists of Art Brut,[13] and Porret-Forel and Dubuffet would remain integral parts of each other's lifelong research endeavors.

Porret-Forel writes in a catalogue essay in *Comme un papillon sur Elle* that Aloise "became very fond of Dubuffet, as he was of her ... he was very sweet with her. When they talked together I think they understood each other quite well."[14] Dubuffet's fascination with madness and *art chez les fous* lead him to opine, problematically, that Aloïse was indeed quite lucid, and that those who were considered insane had in some part chosen to allow for this slippage from a common reality into their alternate, inner reality. Needless to say, the doctors Steck and Poret-Forel differed from Dubuffet on this point, but Dubuffet's interest encouraged their appreciation for Aloïse' artistic practice.

---

12   Thévoz, a professor and art historian, was the first director of the Art Brut Collection in Lausanne.

13   Her first works entered the collection in 1948.

14   Porret-Forel, *Comme un Papillon sur Elle* (Shiga Prefecture, Japan: Hareyari-Kumottari, 2009), 34.

In 1966, Fascicule #7 of the Compagnie de l'Art Brut featured Dubuffet's expansive text "Haut art d'Aloïse" as well as Porret-Forel's text "Aloïse et son théâtre de l'univers," both of which have since been reproduced in subsequent catalogues. Dubuffet's text is a testament to the high esteem in which he held Aloïse; he champions her as one of the most important of his still-developing cache of Art Brut artists. He calls her "a gourmande of abstract ideas, thoughts, transfigurations, signs, symbols and allegories..."[15] and writes that the cultivation of this gourmandise suggests that she indulged herself to the point of provoking a profound disinterest in or ennui with the social rules and workings of everyday life. "Haut art" is interwoven with insight; it is an almost uncanny intuiting of Aloïse's modus operandi and includes examinations of both the life and creations of Aloïse. Dubuffet theorizes Aloïse's process as simultaneously one of self-prescribed psychic rehabilitation, and a sublime indulgence in perpetuating her own madness. In other words, her *traitement-en-oeuvre* further alienated her from the outside world, while at the same time generating a parallel, protective, sur-reality in which her intellect and creativity could fully blossom. "Though some narrative may be perceived from one page to the next, the absence of any continuous logic frees her oeuvre from such banal requirements," writes Dubuffet. "It insists on timelessness, impermanence, and irrationality as rules, rather than as exceptions."[16] Dubuffet suggests that the structure of Aloïse's universe might be irrational, but only inasmuch as it is Aloïse who defines the universal rules, which are formed independently of those by which we commonly abide.

While Dubuffet's text is a primer for comprehending Aloïse's vast oeuvre and history, in relation to his impressions of the artist herself, Porret-Forel's text illuminates the intricacies of this other-universe in even greater detail. "Aloïse et son théâtre" sets about the task of decrypting the super-subjective logic integral to Aloïse's drawings and writings. Porret-Forel now begins to decode Aloïsian hieroglyphics within the framework Dubuffet laid out in the *Fascicules*. Yet unlike Dubuffet, Porret-Forel's engagement with the artist did not supercede the visibility of the work itself; she did not fold Aloïse's narrative into

---

15   Jacqueline Porret-Forel & Jean Dubuffet, "Haut Art d'Aloïse," *Fascicule de l'Art brut N°7* (Lausanne: Compagnie de l'Art Brut,1966).

16   *Ibid.*

the formation of another, larger one. Art Brut, a worthy initiative, and incredible concept, nevertheless supplanted the individual artists' histories and works with its excess of cultural significance and its art-historical agenda.[17]

CONTEMPORARY ART BRUT HISTORIANS

"Distance in time is actually a productive possibility of understanding."[18] From my perspective, Aloïse's practice took place in the past, as did her interactions with Jacqueline, as did the latter's analytical work. Taking into account the distance between then and now, it's possible to overcome the temporal distance between my text, myself, and those two. Accommodating this space requires a participative reading of Jacqueline and Aloïse, meaning that in order to place those texts, some comprehension of the times in which they wrote (what they'd have read, places they saw, social climates they'd lived in) is necessary. While historical distancing allows for the reader/writer to honestly attempt objectivity, from this posterior perspective, overcoming that distance—the alienness of the texts—also means founding a new interpretation. This act of interpreting another's writing means reading in relation to what one already knows. This ultimately appropriates some of the meaning of the text, spiriting it away from the author's original intent, but it is an absolutely necessary step toward beginning to understand the text. If one imagines both Porret-Forel's and Aloïse's texts as mute interlocutors of sorts—mute for their incapacity to argue against interpretation—the secondary text endeavors to engage with them based on the knowledge attained of each author.

Jacqueline Porret-Forel's search for meaning, in reading Aloïse's texts and drawings and in formulating a system for decryption, was an effort

---

17 One might look, for comparison, to the early history of the Museum of Modern Art (MoMA) in New York, which includes "Self-Taught Art" as part of its original directive. The 1938 show *Masters of Popular Painting: Modern Primitives of Europe and America* was a landmark exhibition and enormously generative for art historical discourse (consider the ongoing importance of the terms "Self Taught," "Naïve," and "Outsider" art), but it nevertheless prioritized MoMA's agenda and legacy over those of the individual artists represented.

18 Barry Smith, "Distanciation and Textual Interpretation," *Laval théologique et philosophique* (Université Laval: V.43 #2 June 1987), 207.

to understand both the author and the works. The resultant writing of this search, what Hans Gadamer calls "the mediation of comprehension by way of explanation,"[19] synthesized her research through the process of exteriorizing it. In turn, the rearticulated synthesis of her research refined her character sketches into fuller portraits of Aloïse. Writing about Aloïse for varied fora, with different initiatives, and over the course of several decades of her life, meant revising and re-revising her language. Through these revisions and reconsiderations of how to best describe Aloïse, a deeper knowledge of her subject was attained and a richer portrait generated. Her process was neither reductive nor additive, it simply revealed an architecture already in place, if buried. Pinning as many metaphors to signs as possible, one could say Porret-Forel took the "ir" out of "irrational."

The act of transcribing Aloïse' writings into a language more readily readable introduced a level of clarity to the oeuvre, both for the doctor and for subsequent readers. For the reader of Jacqueline's and Aloïse's writings, the task is one of interpretation—of the authors and texts and their functions in tandem. Porret-Forel's mediation of her compiled research afforded access to Aloïse through French language only.[20] And Aloïse's writings have not been previously published in English translation.

The task of a secondary historian is slippery, and my objective was manifold: First, to more clearly understand the meanings of the individual words and their implications within both authors' texts. To this end, I translated much of their writing into my native tongue. Second, to attempt a translation of Aloïse's writing based on the analytic structures set in place by Porret-Forel, out of respect for the doctor's ordering. Finally, to account for the further distanciation by linguistic translation—though the words and phrases have been carefully translated, maintaining as much Aloïsian nuance as possible, understanding the meaning of the text remains elusive.

All writings have meanings that endure time, translations, and interpretations. The essence of a text, or ideality of meaning, persists, despite different interpretations by differently motivated persons.

---

19   *Ibid.*, 211.
20   Until the 2009 publicatoin of *Aloïse: Comme un papillon sur Elle*.

This atemporal existence within the text, which is neither the author's original intended meaning, nor the ideal meaning to be derived by the original intended reader, is something that remains comprehensible and open to participation. It's a reassuring idea, certainly, that what's to be found within the text remains ever-visible, despite one's intentions in delving in. For this reason, I've supplied tools for setting about reading Aloïse in English, but my interpretation of her texts themselves remains absent. As Aloïse was initially mediated by Jacqueline, all mediating here is also through Jacqueline.

If one assumes that it is neither possible to divine Aloïse's original intention in writing nor the writing's intended meaning, it is nevertheless possible to examine that enduring meaning inherent in the texts themselves. Interpretations performed in the absence of the author's clear intention produce myriad meanings. As one reads with and for what one already knows, associating actively with the shimmering visible bits one finds within the text, one forges a personal relationship to it and an interpretation is formed. But it's immediately apparent in reading Aloïse that these texts were not intended for another's eyes. There's no evidence that we are her intended reader, and even letters addressed to particular persons don't seem to include the addressee as intended reader. It's uncanny, the feeling of reading as unsolicited voyeur. Aloïse's writings address an audience of one and therefore the writer's intention and the meaning to be gleaned by the intended reader are safely nestled together—like two facing mirrors. And if there is no extra-Aloïsian audience to be divined within the writing, there is therefore no intended meaning for said intended audience to extract.[21]

---

21   This is not "diaristic" writing, written to oneself—rather, the interlocutor is internal. Aloïse is like many other Art Brut or Outsider artists in this way.

GENESIS

In creating the world anew, Aloïse drew what she saw and heard: the personages, places, flora, and fauna populating her universe presented themselves to her so that they might be named and called into being. The world appeared before her and she learned its language, uttering it for the first time as she marked its existence onto paper. If the sign (the drawing or writing) and its signifier (the imagined) are formed symbiotically, then drawing an image on paper (the representation of a thing envisioned) is akin to naming it. Transposing signs in written and drawn form, Aloïse identified them and made them knowable in her language.

In Genesis, God calls lightness, darkness, the earth, the seas, and the heavens into existence with His word, investing in each creature and plant a *name,* endowing each with identity. As He installs names—the language of nature—within things, He makes it possible for them to be known. Thereafter man, in his divine creativity, understanding this mute language of the natural world, completes God's work by speaking the name of each thing in human word.

> *And out of the ground the LORD God formed every beast of the field, and every fowl of the air; and brought them unto Adam to see what he would call them: and whatsoever Adam called every living creature, that was the name thereof.*

Calling out to all living things, Adam derives their names from what he understands them to be. Walter Benjamin writes, "God's creation is completed when things receive their names from man, from whom in name language alone speaks."[1] By giving human word to things, man is able to fully attain *knowledge* of them. The *naming* of everything by man is an act of reverse transfiguration—that which was created of divine knowledge and divine word is transformed into that which exists in human knowledge and of human word. Aloïse's universe is also fashioned in this Edenic manner. It is born of her innate knowledge of things, and called into being through a process of divining the essence of those things and naming them accordingly.

NAMING/NOUNING

Name is the "heritage of human language." It is created from the knowledge invested by God, coupled with the creative act performed by man: "The name is that *through* which and *in* which, language communicates itself absolutely."[2] Man's early existence in the book of Genesis was one of *immediate entity,* wherein he communicated wordlessly and directly with God, and all other things. This community of the created world was "immediate and finite," thus nameable and fathomable.

In *Écrit sur une feuille de papier d'argent*, Aloïse records things, places, and persons as they appear to her. Actions transpire, but all the

---

1 Walter Benjamin, "On Language as Such and on the Language of Man," trans. E. Jephcott, in *Reflections: Essays, Aphorisms, Autobiographical Writings*, ed. Peter Demetz (New York: Schocken, 1986), 65.
2 Ibid., 65.

elements are disconnected—they are germinal beings: *Manteau, sphinx of Rumine, coronation of Napoleon, Coppet, brodequin of Thalie, "marriages under flowered arches," parade floats, Ceres, "immolated dove on the altar," the ban of Lygie, the Bon Enfant.*[3] Since those first figures appeared identical to those found in *the ancient world of other times*, she speaks (writes) the names for them in their native language: she borrows the language of God's creation to populate her own universe. The forms are transfigured from their 'ancient world' existences by their inclusion in Aloïse's universe, but their characters aren't yet activated. *Écrit* was composed during what Porret-Forel has called Aloïse's "autistic" period. During this time, her drawings and writings simply catalogued her universe's central elements. In later works, the characters in *Écrit* reappear, reanimated. Aloïse catalyzes their animation by distilling the attributes of things down to abstracted signs and then redistributing those properties. But in this early stage, things are simply called into existence by being named, thus known, to Aloïse.

After his eviction from the Garden, man fashions language into a *means* of communication. When it falls into the service of man, *name's* primary function ceases to be its immediate connection to the word of God and to the identity of things. According to Benjamin, the origin of abstraction, or the pure sign, was introduced by the un-nameable and therefore unfathomable abstraction of God's Judgment. With the Fall from Eden, and the subsequent creation of good and evil, Judgment exceeds the limits of nameable and knowable things, and therefore exists exclusively in the realm of the divine and ineffable.

And so, man turns away from immediacy, from the contemplation of things' origins and the divination of God's name for them, and creates signs. A language formed purely of signs allows him to more readily place things in the service of his linguistics, but ultimately opens the door to linguistic confusion. Man's expulsion from the language of origins leads inexorably to the fall of the tower of Babel and the subsequent multiplication of languages. This new multiplicity of languages, based on the expressive needs of diverse peoples who translate the signs and not the essence of things themselves, results in the over-naming of things: "signs become confused where things are

---

3   See lexicon for more information on each of these terms.

entangled..."[4] In the post-Babelian fissioning of language, the process of creating signs out of signifiers becomes a form of abstraction. Signs created from other signs attempt the divine perfection of the pure sign through an effort to completely detach themselves from a direct link to the knowable, visible world. A linguistic sign modeled directly after another linguistic sign bypasses the association to any *thing* and therefore has no tangible corollary. In short, after Babel, language becomes self-referential.

But Aloïse's act of naming does not partake of these post-Babelian vicissitudes. First, because it is not born of her expressive needs: it is the adaptation of language to speak within an existence transfigured. She names not for the sake of facilitating communication, but in order to articulate a thing's existence in the language in which she recalled it to mind. Second, the Aloisian idiom is formed of a creative process of fusioning rather than fissioning. Babelian fissioning creates excess signs for things, as well as signs for those germinal signs; Aloïsian idiomatic production retains the germinal significance of those signs and expands their potential. As her universe develops autonomy, signs take on a multiplicity of signifiers.

In the progression from earlier to later work, one can see Aloïse's language become known to her. As she learned it, the figures and *things* of her creations ceased to present themselves before her to be named and became instead inhabitants of her world, speaking their presences in the language she gave them. When Aloïse's universe is named and set in motion, abstraction is introduced through metonymy. It's not a postlapsarian abstraction: the names of things become signs for the original referent (the words as they exist in the *ancient world of other times*) and also signifiers of their new functions and values within Aloïsian linguistics. In her text *Billet à l'Inconnue* (1947), many earthly things are transformed through their actions or uncommon associations:

> *a manteau Imperial interwoven in Promethean sphinx*
> *one could say the heavens of Saint Pierre ... has its*
> *brodequin*
> *flowered Campdigolio of Lygie ban ô dove immolated*
> *on the altar of Quo Vadis*

---

4   Benjamin, "On Language," 72.

Aloïsian abstraction, generated through the induction of linguistic transfiguration and the further fusioning of signs, makes accurately translating Aloïse's later writings an elusive task. The words themselves have direct meanings, but the multiplicity of possible associations abstracts them to such a degree that only Aloïse could know their true intended signification. Her personages, places, and things cease to directly correlate to the knowable world of man, as their meanings are a *détournement* of the French language in verse. Aloïse's use of proper nouns incorporates the fractalization of tacit meanings into the potential of the name. Inasmuch as the slippage between nominal-signifier and signified personnage is possible, it catalyzes the simultaneous consideration of attributes of each thing or person conjured. Take the word "Marguerite," for example: the term can mean "daisy"; it can refer to any one of several people known to Aloïse by that name (Marguerite de Bourgogne, Corbaz, Mahaim, Muller...); or it can evoke the child's game of plucking petals off a daisy. Each of these meanings is interwoven into each iteration of this name. While Aloïse may have intended to invoke a specific person, the connection remains uncertain for the reader who must consider all possible associations at once.

Again, augmenting the signifier with an excess of meaning is not a form of linguistic confusion. Rather Aloïse *reads* each thing as it appears in itself and sees that some of these things shall be called with the same name. Apparent metonymy is thrown off kilter, as a proper noun is loaded up with potential—it is all at once many metaphors and that which signals them. The phrase "Yersin of banknote/stamp" offers another example of the name's multiplicity of meaning. The Yersin to which Aloïse refers was probably a doctor at Saint Rosière. Or perhaps it's the famous doctor credited with discovering the bacteria which causes the bubonic plague. Yet another textually synchronous Yersin, also of Swiss origin, was noteworthy for designing images for postage stamps. Accepting that her phrase may conjure up numerous disparate narratives, her text then proposes an affinity between the previously unrelated histories.

The names given to elements recurring throughout Aloïse's work do bear resemblance to things in the *ancient world of other times.* But, through their contact with the *Solar Ricochet,* they are transformed. A characteristic of a particular thing is amplified to the point of becoming its primary identity, making it *seem* unnatural in relation to its conventionally conceived composure; the typically prominent attributes remain either unspoken or subdued traits. A *manteau,* for instance, is identifiable by name but not by its customary purpose (keeping warm), because it performs a function *supernatural* to itself. Since it is foremost a symbol of luxury for Aloïse, the manteau is immediately associated with those worn by Napoleon and Josephine in Raphael's depiction of the coronation.[5] However, in employing this symbol in simile, luxuriousness is then transferred onto other objects, places or actions of decadent qualities. The compositional elements of Aloïsian prose are weightier than those of this world—their multiplicities of meanings add substantial heft.

RESEMBLANCE

In *The Order of Things,* Foucault writes, "the space inhabited by immediate resemblances becomes like a vast open book; it bristles with written signs; every page is seen to be filled with strange figures that intertwine and in some places repeat themselves.... What form constitutes a sign and endows it with its particular value as a sign?—Resemblance does. It signifies exactly in so far as it resembles what it is indicating (that is, a similitude)."[6] According to Foucault, Adam read the language *inscribed on the thing itself,* so the words he spoke to name the thing were *similar* to the things themselves. And like Benjamin before him, Foucault discusses the fissioning of language after Babel, introducing the concept of "similitude" to account for what was lost.

After the fall of Babel and the fissioning of language, a search for meaning through the use of language becomes a reconstructive effort "to bring to light a resemblance" between signs and signifiers. In Aloïse's recreation of language, one sees a related process. In attentively reading all that eidetically appeared before her eyes and in naming each thing anew, Aloïse's search for meaning fostered natural similitudes between the *ancient world of other times* and the things populating the new world. The unsolicited reader navigating the multitudinous and

---

5   See the lexicon, part 1, "Aloïse's Universe: Foundation Words"—in particular "Solar Ricochet," "Le Sacre de Napoleon," and "*manteau.*"

6   Michel Foucault, *The Order of Things* (London: Routledge, 1970), 59. The French-language edition dates to 1966.

seemingly ambiguous relations of signs to signifiers in these texts must search for the metonymic connections to opera, personages in European history and literature, and verse mis/appropriated from a plenitude of sources. Thereafter, the task is that of deciphering their transfigured states within the text.

According to Muriel Edelstein, it is not uncommon for schizophrenics to create their universes anew, beginning in what they perceive to be an ancient time, or the beginning of civilization. The manifestations of this re-creation often have their roots in religious texts. This is the case with Aloïse. She weaves her metonymic matrix anew at the dawn of all creation, as Eve, as Earth, embodying and propagating all that comes after. The underlying system of generative mechanics at work in Aloïsian creation is a metaphysical one, influenced by mysticism, religion, and alchemy.

Benjamin writes, "The language of nature is comparable to a secret password that each sentry passes to the next in his own language, but the meaning of the password is the sentry's language itself."[7] He suggests here that nothing is communicated *through* language, that a written or spoken language itself communicates nothing, and that words themselves are simply empty content, purely symbolic of other things and other actions. But things can be communicated *in* language—meaning that language is a vehicle for content, rather than the content itself. Accepting both of these ideas, it stands to reason that within every language exists an infinity of potential signs and an infinity of ways to communicate them. All that is signified in language limits its own potential to be articulated, and that which remains unperceived remains inexpressible. Through the action of searching for meaning, seeking resemblances through word, all that was previously invisible to language becomes knowable. Interpreting Aloïse's text is a process of learning her unique grammatical rules and her terminology. The *language* relating one thing to another exposes the logic of their relation.

"The grammar of beings is an exegesis of these things," writes Foucault, and the difficulty in interpretation lies in the potential for eisegesis. *Exegesis,* or attempting an objective search for the meaning imbedded

---

7   Benjamin, "On Language," 74.

in a text, finds its antithesis in *eisegesis,* a *false* reading of a text in which the subjective interpretation obscures the text's true meaning. While language expresses that which is communicable and relevant in each era, it also identifies that which is omitted and inarticulable. In Foucault's concise formulation, "everything is said in every age." The factors conditioning an age, giving every era its style, its trends, and its values, direct the formation of the language used in that era. That which is socio-temporally relevant in each age is *visible* and productive of the language describing it. As a result, what remains unsaid illustrates the negative spaces within a culture.

In translating and researching the historically significant proper names, and thus further decrypting Aloïse's writing, it becomes apparent that there is ample opportunity for both exegesis and eisigesis. For example, the phrase "Château de Montaulieu (de Beaulieu)" in *À Mademoiselle Rosine* suggests the existence of a castle called Monteaulieu at a place called Beaulieu. And while such a place may exist, within the context of her other writings, one guesses that "Montaulieu" is most likely the residence of Madame *Montolieu*. Madame Isabelle de Montolieu was a writer and translator, and a Vaudoise of the same epoch and literary clique as Madame de Staël (the one-time inhabitant of the chateau de Beaulieu, in Lausanne). In this example, then, temporal and cultural propinquity[8] (historical proximity) form a basis for potential association. What's more, in Madame Montolieu's text "Les Châteaux Suisses: anciennes anecdotes et chroniques"[9] there is a discussion of Madame de Staël's residence at Beaulieu. This adds an additional layer to an already complex cosmos: the "château de Montaulieu (de Beaulieu)" then also references the castle of the text and brings to light a relationship between the texts of two authors who were contemporaries. In the contact created by realizing the resemblance between two things, we can perceive the previously-hidden reason for their now-apparent affinity—an attribute that is only revealed in conceiving of the things together. Thus, the resemblance both unveils the basis of their propinquity and suggests that we must hunt for it.

---

8   Propinquity is temporal as well as spatial proximity, and can refer to the microcosmic space within the macrocosmic, the nanosecond within longtime.

9   Isabelle Montolieu, *Les Châteaux Suisses: anciennes anecdotes et chroniques* (Lausanne: Samuel Blanc, 1865).

Propinquity is not the only form of resemblance—similarities can also be found at great distance. For instance: the stars in her eyes resemble the celestial diamonds imprinted on the firmament. Or, a great imperial manteau spread to protect, to glorify, and to display royal beauty resembles God's manteau spread across the night sky in all its majesty. In the latter case, the seemingly imitative relationship is the product of a similarity in *function*. The difficulty in decoding or translating the emulative relationships arises where one thing so closely resembles another that a natural sort of twinship is formed—when it becomes difficult to discern the original entity from its mirror. These twin entities seem to be formed symbiotically *as* each other's mirrors, or they result from a loss of ability to discern the original from the duplicate. Foucault's description of this entangled twinship, in the function he calls *emulation*, and Aloïse's description of *Ricochet Solaire* are remarkably similar:

> [*Man's*] *inner sky may remain autonomous and depend only upon itself, but on condition that by means of his wisdom, which is also knowledge, he comes to resemble the order of the world, takes it back into himself and thus recreates in his inner firmament the sway of that other firmament in which he sees the glitter of the visible stars. If he does this, then the wisdom of the mirror will in turn be reflected back to envelop the world in which it has been placed; its great ring will spin out into the depths of the heavens, and beyond; man will discover that he contains 'the stars within himself ... , and that he is thus the bearer of the firmament with all its influences.*[10]

> *That sleeping earth, inert, is awakened by the grand celestial bell with its stars, fertilized by the touch of the sun's rays that fall upon it and cause it to spout forth in ricochet, a multitude of images ... immorally famished in the night, beneath the triple astral bouquet, the tree of life, that fuses the flesh of an earthen urn of gold*

---

10 Foucault, *The Order of Things*, 23.

caressed with a dash of passion of the celestial plows of
the flowers of its body which it sows.[11]

The Ricochet Solaire is a fusing function; it brings together previously disparate elements. Take the references to the cosmos, for instance. The cosmos is metaphorically likened to carpets spanning the ceiling of the sky; the celestial bodies are likened to stones, *pierres*. Here, emulation is reversible; the physical beings of the stars and the heavens are compared to earthly creations, while the word "pierres" takes on all the grandeur of the firmament. The example of celestial bodies likened to pierres, further decrypted, provides a fascinating instance of the conjoining of signifiers. Probably unapparent to most readers, and possibly unintended by the writer, it furnishes depth within the text. If *p/Pierre* can be read as stone (whether precious or utile), then the additional association to Saint Peter (Saint Pierre)—Christ's chief disciple and the pillar upon which the Christian church was founded—at once infuses all mention of "stone" with Peter's story. At the same time, the association links Saint Peter to a humble and ubiquitous raw material. And given that many of Aloïse's references come from secondary texts or from illustrations, a mention of Saint Peter brings with it a range of representations of his image. Thus, representations of Saint Peter in painting, in verse, and in churches named for him, offer an even greater field of reference on which Aloïse might draw when making a connection with "pierre."

Even more curious than this entangled twinship are the *analogous* relationships within Aloïse's texts. These differ from metonymous associations in that the things connected don't possess similar identities: a connection by analogy forces their association and the consideration of their similarity. This is further complicated by the fact that Aloïse vacillates between asserting metaphors and constructing similes, between saying that the heavens *are* a manteau and that the heavens *are like* a manteau. In an association by simile, the qualities of two or more things are conjured up for comparison; in metaphor, Aloïse asserts that one thing *is* another, possessing all its qualities and sharing its identity. In this vacillation, the original is revealed as an image mirrored in simile, and reburied again through metaphor.

---

11   Aloïse Corbaz cf. Jacqueline Porret-Forel, *Aloïse et le théâtre de l'univers* (Genève: Éditions d'Art Albert Skira, 1993), 104.

In its most resplendent iteration, an analogy results from a mixed metaphor—one history is conjured up in a word, but is *détourné*, or hijacked, by another history, which also points to that same word. In *À Mademoiselle Rosine,* there are several examples of this, for instance: "...the Alps like a pedestal of gilded granite in the blue sky = its human-like floes face of Napoleon risen on earth," and "modern Joan of Arc nude (the red Catherine on a horse) ... in the cords of the banner of brocade." The mixed metaphor, or the malapropism—the free creation of analogies—ushers in an entire universe of images and narratives in the redistribution of signifiers to signs.

Aloïse' use of *en* (as, in), *à* (at, on, for, to, of the), and *de* (from, of) pose a very particular problem for the translator. Often these words are used to create simile, but just as often they are meant as posses-sives or should be translated strictly as prepositions. And in translating passages lacking punctuation or capitalization, it's especially difficult to discern which function is intended in each instance. *Diamants à la Marie Louise* could translate to "diamonds to Marie Louise," "Marie Louise diamonds," or "diamonds in the fashion of Marie Louise."

Or, the phrase: "She did not remain like a cypress upon the tomb of humanity" (*"elle ne restait pas comme un cyprès sur le tombeau d'humanité"*). Here, *she* does not perform an action like that of a cypress, although the action she doesn't perform (remaining on the tomb), which is linked to the cypress, is not the characteristic most closely associated with a cypress (although the branches of the cypress tree are used in some mourning rituals). In the same fashion, the *tomb of humanity* is not a tomb-like humanity, rather, humanity forms its own tomb.

Or, "...the floral wreath of the royal earth ... that opens in flower show-ing its *manteaux*" (*"couronne de la terre royale ... qui s'ouvre en fleur étale ses manteaux"*). "Manteaux" can be read as luxuriousness, richness, and bounty, rather than as a literal overcoats. As this word is often paired with *imperial, royal, majestic,* in the absence of such descriptors, manteaux alone implies them. And so the manteau, transformed from its natural coat-like state, implies the richness of the vernal verdure, or the scent thereof, or the energy of nature spread across the land.

In becoming signifiers through the process of fusing or fusioning of meaning, oftentimes the multiples forfeit their individual identities in identification with the whole. Those aspects which are not necessarily the most unique to the individual take priority in their identification with a larger whole; that which is similar and was less prominent becomes the identifiable characteristic, and as it is shared with (similar to) a twin, it is identified in association with its twin. It was stated above that Aloïse's (re)namings often resulted in sussing out characteristics of a thing that are either not immediately apparent or not normally attributed to that thing, and then naming (transfiguring) them on the basis of this new meaning. Her metonymic use of names, especially proper names, ties her language to the *ancient world of other times.* In the process of transfiguration, the signified lose some of their immediate association with common things and are instead set in relation with each other. Therefore, the signification of each named thing is understood first in relation to its transfigured state (within the text and to its contents), and second in relation to its original reference.

Many words and phrases are left intact in the original French for exactly this reason. In these cases, their cultural and linguistic specificity, or their usage as proper names is the primary signification.[12] There are a few special cases where an impossible translation—one in which the linguistic specificity of the verse prevents an accurate translation to English—was nonetheless translated. In these cases, the *jeu-de-mots,* the pun, is specific to early 20th century French and is détourné by Aloïsian malapropism. For example *"donner un bouquet à quelqu'un"* (to give someone a bouquet), is an expression of cordiality. In translation, this double-entendre is lost, though one can still accept that giving flowers to someone is a pleasantry. In another example involving "bouquet," Aloïse liases the words *auto* and *bouquet,* and the result sounds very much like *auto-da-fé.* And the phrase "bouquet finale," meaning the finale of a fireworks show, is sometimes re-versed as "banquet finale." The play of "bouquet" is of course just one of the many untranslatable jeux-de-mots to be found within Aloïse's verse. The following is a partial list of such plays on words.

---

12   Each of these instances is translated in the lexicon. For example: the phrases *Sans-souci* (carefree, or the Prussian château and vacation home of Kaiser Wilhelm), *Saint-Esprit* (Marie de la Charité du St. Esprit, or any church of this name, or "The Holy Ghost"), *Saint-Ange* or *Michel Ange* (Saint Angel or places bearing his name, and Saint Michael or Michaelangelo, or places with his name).

le beau monde[1]	the beautiful people	very beautiful ladies
les prendre au berceau	to take them from the cradle	cradle-robbing, flirting with someone too young
du blé	some wheat	monnied, prosperous
les brodequins	the boots	a type of torture
se serrer la ceinture	to tighten one's belt	poverty, need
chant des sirènes	siren song	mystification, lure
le jeu de Cipris	Cyprus's game	sexual connotation
l'aigle n'engendre point la colombe	the eagle never begets the dove	*maxim*
un coup de marteau	a hammer blow	to be a bit crazy or maniacal
un coup de soleil	a sunburn, sunstroke	to be half-drunk
un coup de verre	a shotglass	a mole or pimple on one's face
recevoir un coup de soleil	to be hit by a ray of sunshine	to fall in love
déchirer la toile	to tear the cloth	to be noisy, like the army or make army/brigade fire
donner le bouquet à quelqu'un	to give the bouquet to someone	fond welcome, cordiality
san étoile commence à blanchir	his/her star begins to fade	the fall of someone of influence

---

1   The bold type indicates which word is mentioned in Aloïse's text. In the cases where an entire phrase is boldened, the entire phrase can be found in her text. It is uncertain whether she intended to reference these sayings, however they were part of her era's common parlance and must have been considered in forming her jeu-de-mots.

*il ne s'est pas fait **déchirer le manteau***	he did not tear his manteau	he did not pray
faire du genou	to play 'knees'	to flirt, to allure someone
faire une fleur	make a flower	generosity, a favor, present
fil d'Ariane	thread of Ariane	the underlying thread
*avoir un **front d'airain***	to have a bronze forehead	audacity, aplomb, «to have steel shorts»
jouer des orgues	play the organ	Sexual connotation
*pendre son **manteau** à faible cheville*	to wear an ankle-length coat	ill-fated, barking up the wrong tree
*petit **manteau** bleu*	little blue *manteau*	goodwill/benevolence
*quitter le **manteau***	to take off one's *manteau*	to slouch
*sous le **manteau***	under the *manteau*	in secret
*garder les **manteaux***	to keep/guard the *manteau*	to be private/secreted
*avec des si, on **mettrait** Paris en **bouteille***	with the ifs one could put Paris in a bottle	with so many ifs anything is possible an impossibility
*feindre d'aimer est pire qu'être faux **monnayeur***	feigning love is worse than being a counterfeiter	*maxim*
monter à l'arbre	climb the tree	to be duped, the pigeon, screwed
monter à l'échelle	climb the ladder	to be swindled, fall into a trap
*une **muette** des halles*	an army/mute of the halls	a bossy, insolent, foul-mouthed woman
être à l'ombre	to be in the shadows	to be in prison, seclusion
*une vie de **pacha***	a pasha's life	to live like a lord, luxuriously

*à Pâques ou à la **Trinité***	at Easter or the Trinity	unforeseen or very uncertain
pauvre d'esprit	small-spirited	imbicile, impertinent, sot
*je l'ai vu **aux prunelles***	I looked it in the eyes	happenstance, coincidence, occurence
raser les murs	to raze the walls	hiding to escape reprisals
*c'est la **toile** de **Pénélope***	it's Penelope's cloth	to continue to occur infinitely
quant-à-moi	according to me	to have the last word, arrogance, insolence
*être **entre quatre murs***	to be between four walls	closed in (voluntarily or involuntarily), sequestered
*recevoir quelqu'un **bras dessus bras dessous***	welcome someone arm in arm	fond welcome, cordiality
*C'est la chanson du **Ricochet***	It's the song of the Ricochet	repetitive talk/action, ad infinitum
*voir tout en **rose***	to see everything rose-colored	to live comfortably
*être sur un **lit de roses***	to be on a bed of roses	ravishment, ecstasy, enchantment, perfection
*être comme une **rosière***	to be like a rosary	virginity, chasteness
*une voix de **sirène***	a siren's voice	an enchanteress
*jouer sur **deux tableux***	to play on two tables	cunnery, craftiness
*être **sur les genoux***	to kneel	lassitude, exhaustion
*faire **valser***	to make waltz	to overhwelm with blows/ insults to repudiate/reject

"Translation is a removal from one language into another language through a continuum of transformations. Translation passes through continua of transformation, not abstract areas of identity or similarity," writes Benjamin. But those abstract areas of identity and similarity contain the meaning (the sense) of the words themselves. As early 20th century Swiss French was transformed into Aloïsian idiom, the particularities of language were re-abstracted, and neologisms and malapropisms formed in the process. Though an accurate translation of Aloïsian to contemporary English may in fact be impossible, the idea of *an accurate translation* limits the terms and possibilities of translation itself—it discourages any transformation. In translating verse, one hopes to capture its essence (those abstract areas) through intuiting its sense. Intuiting the essence of Aloïsian texts is very much *la chanson du ricochet*, or *un tonneau de Danïades*, or *la toile de Pénélope*. Rereading and retranslating Aloïse might reveal an infinity of metonymic relations, in a self-contained and self-generating nimbus of linguistic creation. In a recent interview, Jacqueline Porret-Forel revealed that she'd just recently learned that the process of the *solar ricochet* is very similar to, and possibly modeled after, that of photosynthesis. These ongoing epiphanies, *ad infinitum*, tempt one to delve further into Aloïse's universe in an effort to fully understand it, in an attempt to produce an "accurate translation." But as these revelations are seemingly infinite, the task remains seductively elusive.

My sincerest gratitude goes to everyone who assisted in the creation
of this work.

I cannot find the words to   my editor
Amiel Melnick, and to Steffani Jemison, series editor, who made this
publication possible.

For translation editing:
Marina Rodrigues
Emmanuel Dayan
Aurèle Ferrier
Céline Muzelle
Solkem N'Gangbet

For additional support:
Laurent Danchin
Muriel Edelstein
Vincent Monod
John Ollman
Lucienne Peiry
Jacqueline Porret-Forel

Foundational support:
La Fondation Aloïse Corbaz
La Collection de l'Art Brut
La Cité Internationale des Arts
The Joan Mitchell Foundation

for: joan tom taylor jordan

ISBN: 978-0-9833815-0-1

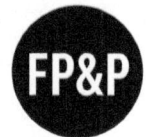

future plan and program

Future Plan and Program
http://futureplanandprogram.com

Please direct inquiries to:
thefuture@futureplanandprogram.com

Book editor: Amiel Melnick
Series editor: Steffani Jemison
Series designer: Sebastian Civarolo

Future Plan and Program was incubated in 2010-2011 by Project Row Houses.

Acknowledgements: Danielle Burns, Justin Cavin, Aisen Chacin, Ashley Clemmer-Hoffman, Cheryl Flores, Quincy Flowers, Hannah Ireland, Philip Jemison, Steven Jemison, Hannah Ireeland. Rick Lowe, Jasmine Jamillah Mahmoud, Phyllis McCallum, Solkem N'Gangbet, Michael Peranteau, Nikki Pressley, Linda Shearer, Martine Syms, Michael Kahlil Taylor, and Julie Thomson.

Future Plan and Program was generously funded in part by the following individuals: Kerry Inman & Denby Auble, John Roberson & John Blackmon, Danielle Antoinette Burns, Justin Cavin, Jereann Chaney, Melody Clark, Ashley Clemmer Hoffman & Brendan Hoffman, Phyllis L. McCallum and Steven Jemison, Joey Romano & Nicole Laurent, Victoria Thomas McGhee, Scott Sawyer & Michael Peranteau, Gregory & Diane Schultz, Leigh & Reggie Smith, and Rebecca Trahan. Special thanks to Jill Whitten & Robert Proctor.

Funding for Steffani Jemison's residency at Project Row Houses was provided by: The National Endowment for the Arts, the City of Houston through the Houston Arts Alliance, Houston Endowment Inc., The Brown Foundation, The Kresge Foundation, The Andy Warhol Foundation for the Visual Arts, and the Texas Commission on the Arts. Steffani Jemison's residency was part of a collaboration with the Core Program at the Glassell School of Art of the Museum of Fine Arts Houston.

234